SAFARI, *R.S.V.P.*

SAFARI, R.S.V.P.

By WILLIAM D. HOLMES

Coward McCann, Inc.　　New York

This book is respectfully dedicated to all members of the East African Professional Hunters Association and in particular to the men and women of Ker and Downey Safaris Limited, who first introduced me to the beauty of Africa.

PREFACE

Each sport has its pinnacle of success. Every sportsman has a goal somewhere in the back of his mind. Perhaps it is only a dream, unknown to all but the dreamer. Others have a determined drive to achieve active participation in the unchallenged "main event" of their chosen sport. The sport of hunting is no different and an African safari is the ultimate goal for most every sportsman. Over three thousand men (and women) hunters will go on safaris during the current year. For each of them it will be an unforgettable experience. A few, perhaps, will be disappointed; but the overwhelming majority will find that Africa is all they hoped it would be and more.

Only a small percentage of these three thousand hunters have been to Africa before. Most have little realization of what Africa is or what to expect on a safari. Many have had little actual experience hunting dangerous game. When there is disappointment concerning Africa or safari life, it is usually the result of misconception. People dream and plan for their one big hunting trip to Africa. They form preconceived opinions of what the country, the game, and the hunting will

9

be. When reality does not conform to these opinions, they feel somehow cheated—even when the reality surpasses their opinions.

I have always felt that more should be written about the actual process of setting up and going on a safari, and of the Big Five—the main trophies that men go to Africa to hunt. As one might guess, this book is my approach to the problem. It is my sincere wish that it serve as an aid to those planning an African safari.

CONTENTS

Illustrations will be found following page 64

SAFARI, *R.S.V.P.*

CHAPTER I

SAFARI,
R.S.V.P.

In Africa any trip is called a safari, whether you visit a neighbor for a weekend or take a hunting trip for several months. The dictionary, however, maintains that a safari is "a journey or hunting expedition in eastern Africa."

I should like to narrow that definition even further, for Kenya and Tanganyika are among the few strongholds left for hunting wild game in Africa. Eastern Africa for me means British East Africa. It has the best safari agencies in the world; the best professional hunters available; it is easily accessible by land and sea from the United States and Europe, and it has the greatest variety of animals for the hunter and photographer. No place else offers such enormous opportunities for success in safariing with such a minimum of inconveniences. Moreover, the city of Nairobi, capital of Kenya, is close to good game grounds and this is the ideal place to start an expedition. I can guarantee there is almost no problem in big-game hunting that has not been settled by the agencies and shops of that city.

"How did you happen to go on a safari?" That is the question most often asked the sportsman just back from Africa.

The answer is, of course, that at some time in his life, the sportsman came down with a bad case of safari fever. He began to dream about hunting big game, he had visions of treks across the veld, he beheld tusks and trophies on his walls, he was sure he would be equal to any challenge of the forest— but perhaps he wasn't quite sure, he wanted to test himself.

At length, he wrote a letter of inquiry to a safari firm.

In the old days, an expedition into the interior was an enormous undertaking. Guides and porters were often difficult to locate; horses, mules, and hunting dogs were expensive, subject to sickness, and often balky; camp equipment and foodstuffs were primitive in the extreme. Of course game was more plentiful than today, but the time and expense of getting to Africa and going out to track down a trophy were so prohibitive that safaris were considered the privileged play of the leisured rich.

Nowadays, certain sports, sites, and situations are no longer for just the privileged few. The dreams are being spread around. Anyone can daydream about bagging a lion or stalking an elephant and find that the dream can be translated into reality. Today, the average safari outlay is not much more than for a thirty-day jaunt to London, Paris, Rome, and Tangiers. Photographic tours are downright inexpensive and every safari firm can suggest a hunting or photographic itinerary in line with the bulk of your pocketbook.

The initial letter of inquiry establishes what type of safari you are interested in and what amount of money you have to invest, how much time you can spend in the bush, the number of people in your party, and the animals you are particularly interested in hunting or photographing.

The answer, then, to "How did you happen to go on a safari?" is "I wrote a letter."

In no time whatsoever you find yourself en route to Africa, about to put your expectations to the test of experience.

Nairobi, a modern city of neat white buildings, has a population of more than a hundred thousand people. Department stores, hotels, office buildings, all the comforts of an up-to-date modern city, are to be found within a few minutes' walk from the principal hotels, the New Stanley and the Norfolk. The center of town swarms with traffic, Indians, Africans, European settlers and safari clients, all rubbing elbows with one another. It is a far cry from imaginings of a rough bush safari town.

I don't think you'll find much else different from the daydreams you had back home, however. You step from your plane to a warm greeting from the safari firm manager and your white hunter. Immediately the talk plunges into big game, and you are immersed in terms and tongues alien to you, for most of the conversation is a mishmash of English, Swahili, and the hunters' jargon. The firm manager is the unsung hero of your safari, a man who seldom leaves his office, and yet sees that every day of your trek through the interior passes without delay or mishap. His work begins the day he receives your first letter of inquiry and his job does not end until you pack up your trophies and go home. Supplies, hotel accommodations, accounts, cable messages, complaints, mail, and the personal eccentricities of each and every one of his clients are the mainstay of his job.

The white hunter is a man who stands apart from other men. So far as I have been able to ascertain, the stories told about these men are not in the least tinged with myth or awe. They are far less exaggerated than they are underplayed. The professional white hunter's services are absolutely essential, for it is he who is familiar with the trails and habits of all species of game; who can lead your party to the best places to shoot without wasting time; who is an agreeable host around the campfire in the evening, and professional and impressive driving the Land Rover hunting car in the morning—a man upon whose shoulders responsibility sits as easily as the safari hat on his head.

The hunter is familiar with all the game regulations and sees that they are obeyed to the letter. All professional hunters are honorary game wardens. No one shoots at night, no one shoots from the hunting car, no one shoots from within two hundred yards of any vehicle. The duties and responsibilities of the white hunter are so varied and encompassing that one man serves no more than two people on a safari, and in many cases he accompanies only one client.

But his most harrowing job is tracking wounded animals into cover. There is one absolute rule of the professional game hunter: Do not permit a wounded animal to flee. If a client has made an error in shooting and the animal has gone into the brush—wounded, waiting, ready to charge—it is the job of the professional white hunter to follow that animal and see that it is destroyed. You do not let a wounded animal drag itself about to die in torture and you do not take the chance that a wounded animal, no matter how light you may believe the wound, will attack another man.

But the client must be preserved at all costs—no firm builds a business on the disasters of its clients—and it is the professional white hunter, therefore, who must risk his neck and go into cover after the wounded animal. Generally the client waits in the hunting car—no matter how *he* feels—while he watches the white hunter and his gunbearer start into the cover.

I often wonder, however, if the professional white hunter

wouldn't prefer the actual danger of the charge of a wounded animal to the endless questions of his clients the first two or three days of the trip. He patiently and helpfully answers them, often time and again because in your excitement and enthusiasm at being in Africa you forget to listen to his answers. But after a day or two, you begin to assimilate the twelve commandments of the big-game hunter:

1. Buy the best guns you can afford (or rent the best ones) and be sure they are adequate for the job you want them to do. (By and large, *all* first-timers in Africa think guns that are of too light a caliber will do the job.)
2. Choice of weapons is of first consideration to the safari. Be sure you understand your gun and that you know how to use it in all positions and under *all* circumstances.
3. Check out your guns thoroughly before going into the bush.
4. Do not use a faulty weapon under any conditions.
5. Do not stint on ammunition. Cheap ammunition is as dangerous as a risky rifle.
6. If you must follow wounded animals, go slowly. Do not rush under any circumstances. Whenever possible, keep trackers with you. They may see movement, shapes, and signs you may miss. Have your gun ready for instant use. Don't bypass any piece of cover, no matter how small. (Most animals can conceal themselves in nothing. It seems impossible that an enormous elephant or a tawny lion could fade into nothingness in the midst of a few scrub bushes, but such is the case.)
7. Keep an eye on other animals that are in the vicinity. Monkeys and birds, for instance, may remain perfectly still; but if you watch them, you will often see they are

looking at something. That something is undoubtedly the animal you are tracking. Listen to the animal and bird sounds around you. They give warning to both hunter and the pursued animal. Remember, because you are stalking one animal, there is no guarantee you may not be charged by another.

8. No matter how sure you are that an animal you have shot has been killed instantly, never approach an animal without your rifle ready for action. Many times a lion, leopard, rhino, Cape buffalo, or elephant may appear in the final stages of death only to bound up and make at the hunter with lightning speed. The animal has only been stunned by the shot; in an instant, it recovers from its grogginess and is up and in full possession of its powers. More hunters have gotten into trouble by overconfidence and carelessness than by bad aim, poor guns, or misfirings.

9. Do not lose your temper at an animal, a hunter, or an African safari crew member. Anger obscures reason, something a hunter must retain at all costs.

10. Keep your sense of humor. A certain amount of tension and anxiety builds up during any safari. Hunting days have long hours, hunters have bad luck, and tempers may rise. Laughter cures all ills.

11. Alcohol and shooting do not mix.

12. One rule which no hunter, on threat of death, can ignore is that he must not become overconfident with repeated success. It is the hunter who believes he is invincible and has Lady Luck as a constant companion who often ends up in the Nairobi cemetery with that awful one-line inscription I have seen, KILLED BY A LION.

The first two or three days after your arrival are spent at the hotel. This gives you time to look over your weapons, get acquainted with your white hunter, fill out game licenses, order clothing and supplies, and make the final preparations for your safari. During this time, the entire safari crew of Africans, who will spend the next month or two with you, will be getting ready for the departure day.

For two people, the average number of boys and the equipment provided will be:

> 1 or 2 professional hunters (If there are two hunters, then each hunter has his own Land Rover or hunting car.)
>
> 1 five-ton truck for hauling equipment (2 trucks when hunters require refrigerator and more supplies than usual if the safari is longer than 30 days)
>
> A multitude of camp equipment and supplies that I shall describe further in another chapter
>
> 1 personal tent boy for each client
>
> 1 No. 1 camp head boy
>
> 1 cook
>
> 2 cook's assistants
>
> 1 or 2 skinners (2 clients, 2 skinners)
>
> 1 driver per truck
>
> 1 gunbearer per hunter
>
> 1 tracker per hunter and local natives hired in various areas
>
> 6 to 8 porters

The husky camp porters do the heavy labor—load and unload the trucks, stake out each new camp, gather firewood and water, and any other labor duties required to keep the camp running smoothly.

21

The drivers of the safari vehicles are also mechanics, as well they must be, for the African bush is not the place for a long breakdown. They can do magic with bits of wire and pieces of metal. The safari firms provide a minimum of one truck and one hunting car for every two clients.

The mess tent boys assist the cook with the cleaning of utensils and preparation of meals. They also do whatever work is assigned them by the camp's Number One head boy. He is, as you would suspect, the most important African in camp, and he rates the highest pay except, possibly, for a top gunbearer. The Number One boy runs the camp and sees to it that the rest of the safari crew do their jobs; if any problems arise that he cannot handle, he reports them to the professional hunter.

The skinners and gunbearers have perhaps the two most important jobs of the hunting safari. The skinners have been trained since childhood to skin animals properly. They are experts in preserving the hide and head so that they will not rot by the time you return to Nairobi. If your trophies have any flesh or fat left on them and are not properly salted down and dried, they will be ruined.

Your gunbearer is the person with whom you have the closest friendship on your safari. His courage as a tracker is indispensable, and his loyalty and steadfastness often mean the difference between life and death—and I do mean yours. If he were to bolt and run, leaving you without a spare weapon, in the face of the charge of an attacking animal, you would be in serious trouble. If he does not track well, an animal may ambush you before you have a chance to defend yourself.

Moreover, the gunbearer is your constant companion in the bush. His encouragement and praise mean more than anyone else's because he *knows*. The professional hunter points out how to stalk game and helps you to understand the importance of terrain, the elementary points in tracking, the necessity of knowing the habits of the animal you are hunting, and the common sense of keeping your nerve in case of a charge. But the gunbearer constantly reminds you of what you have learned from the hunter. When you miss a shot, he's a natural diplomat. He will blame it on bad luck or poor light, or a tricky perspective. He may even blame the animal. But when you do finally make that perfect shot, he will be more elated than you are, grinning and pounding you on the back, shaking your hand wildly and singing your praises to the sky.

By the way, you tip your safari boys at the end of the trip. How much depends on the length of the trip, the difficulties encountered, the services rendered, and so on; your professional hunter will tell you what is right and generous. Your safari firm manager can also suggest a proper remembrance for the white hunter. Usually, the safari client feels there is really no way he can fully repay a hunter for his "beyond the line of duty" services.

There is nowadays, I suppose, such a thing as roughing it on a safari, but the majority of hunters find they are surrounded by every comfort—air mattresses, soft pillows, clean sheets, mosquito netting, a camp desk, lounge chairs, a hot bath in a canvas tub, portable showers, and latrines—and your personal Number One boy to see that you are properly taken care of.

Safari food is a gourmet's delight. All reputable safari firms see that every tinned delicacy you could possibly want is loaded into the truck; but more exciting of course than the foods you are familiar with are those you taste for the first time—all kinds of wild game birds, antelope chops, gazelle steaks, wild asparagus fresh from the riverbanks near camp, chilled slices of tropical fruit, and varieties of fish abounding in the streams and lakes. In a way, the pleasures of your hunting are also the pleasures of your table. What you shoot is food for the table as well as trophies for your gamebag. This is often more of a problem than it sounds. There are at least twenty safari boys, as well as your own party, to feed, excluding the usual number of local trackers hired on a per diem basis; and providing meat for all these people can sometimes turn out to be quite a task. I have seen twenty men eat over a hundred and fifty pounds of meat at one sitting and be ravenous six hours later.

Safari crews sign on practically for the pleasure alone of eating meat. They are accustomed to a meal, grain, and vegetable diet, and meat has an enormous appeal to them. I remember once we were hunting elephant in Northern Kenya, and almost each day I would shoot a good-sized animal for the boys' dinner. After a while, it struck me they were consuming a tremendous quantity of meat. I knew my safari crew had healthy appetites, but I couldn't believe any twenty men could eat that much meat, no matter how hungry they were. Then I happened to bring back a zebra and Cape buffalo on the same day, almost three thousand pounds of meat. Three days later, I was told the camp needed more meat.

A little private investigation showed the meat was being sold to local villages for a tidy profit. For the next week, I instructed the cook to serve canned rations as the boys' only supply of food. After a week of this diet, I brought back some fresh meat. It lasted longer than even I had hoped.

You hunt during the day—from daylight, really—but I am often asked what you do at night, way out in the bush so far away from civilization. Every night, the camp joins around the short-wave radio to listen to Safari Hour, a program that gives world news, sends out important personal and business messages to men and women hunting in the bush, and advises parties on hunting conditions. After the broadcast, clients and hunters usually gather around the campfire and "talk safari." Sometimes the safari boys provide entertainment. Then there is a good deal of lively singing and dancing; and if members of local tribes visit the camp, there is a lot of good-natured rivalry. If you hand out fresh meat to the visitors, they in turn will thank you with song and dance.

Another question—usually timidly put, but earnestly feared —is what happens to you if you have an accident or fall sick. In the old days, this was a serious problem and many men died on the trail because of improper attention, the distances to a doctor, and lack of antibiotics, penicillin, and other drugs. A bite from a poisonous reptile was fatal. The danger from bacteria infection and blood poisoning was worse than the damage of wounds. The mauling of a lion or leopard was serious in itself, but it almost certainly meant blood poisoning. The trails were many days' hike from a center where a reputable doctor could be reached, and many men died on the way.

Today, the safari kit includes a giant medical chest, and the professional hunter is a man well up on advanced first aid. If the emergency arises, the whole countryside is somehow alerted. It is one of the great mysteries of Africa how fast news travels. And bad news always seems to spread faster than the good (as anywhere else). The authorities immediately dispatch aid and, if necessary, a doctor (who can often be flown in in a matter of hours); most of British East Africa's hunting areas are closely connected by roads, and while some of these seem no more than animal trails, they will permit a courageous driver to get a vehicle through at a fair speed. There are many such volunteers if the need arises.

Part of this is all part of the rare sense of brotherhood one feels out in the bush. The extraordinary thing about this feeling is that it is often based on mutual adversities rather than shared successes. Men tend to forget the things that go well, but they remember only too well when circumstances got beyond them and the odds seemed against them. The friend who does not let one down, the acquaintance who suddenly comes through—these make a tie that is never loosened. The hardships shared searching for an animal under a broiling sky or during the cold nights, the stinging bite of the tsetse fly, the cuts and bruises suffered while plunging through thorn thickets during a chase, thirst and hunger, the breakdown of a truck at a crucial moment, the fear every hunter experiences at certain times—these are the things that cement the safari into a single living unit, men hunting dangerous animals, shooting to the best of their ability, tracking wounded animals who may take their lives, trying to keep cool, backing up a member of the safari in danger, retelling the successes and failures around the campfire at the end of the day.

A man who hunts big game undergoes a change. He comes to respect his enemy, and he lives to follow a set of rules which gives his enemy a fair chance. He does not hunt or hurt indiscriminately; he does not butcher animals, and he loathes himself when he wounds and does not kill an animal; he accepts and fulfills the laws of the hunt, and he is a better person for it.

Every hunter feels fear at some time during the chase. There is always the moment when instinct—blind panic—can overtake the hunter and his one drive is to bolt and run, to save himself. The brave hunter admits this. I do not want to hunt with a man who boasts he has never been afraid, that he has never felt like running. I am more afraid of that man than I am of the man who confesses his fear, acknowledges it, and conquers it. Fright leads to panic and panic is the reason for so many accidents among the hunters of big game.

Go ahead and be afraid; just control it.

Whatever fears you have are half destroyed once you have faced them and behaved as well as you can. This is also a valuable lesson the bush teaches you.

So don't worry, go ahead and start making plans right away.

Put that letter to the safari agency in the post.

THE BIG FIVE

The hunter goes to Africa principally for the Big Five—the leopard, lion, rhinoceros, African Cape buffalo, and elephant; or in Swahili, which you can't help falling into after a few weeks in the bush, *chui, simba, faro, mbogo,* and *tembo.* The Big Five are so named because they are the most dangerous and cunning of all animals to hunt. Professional hunters and sportsmen will argue until the end of time which is *really* the most dangerous, intelligent, wary, and cunning. I think that there is something to be said for each.

No matter how often I come up against one of these five tough customers, I know I am in for a surprise because one thing is for certain: You never know all you need to know. There are certain general rules, of course, but each animal's personality, like that of a person, fluctuates with its mood, disposition, and idiosyncrasies. In the bush, there is no such thing as a rule which is never broken; there is no such thing as an animal which behaves just as it should. You know and you do not know. You are always learning, constantly facing new challenges, always on your mettle to interpret and make new decisions.

Whatever member of the Big Five a person claims as most deadly, his reason is usually inspired by a terrifying experience with that animal. If a man has been mauled by a lion and has escaped the physical wrath of the leopard, Cape buffalo, rhino and elephant, quite naturally he will claim the lion is the most dangerous animal to hunt in Africa. A person with leopard claw marks on his throat and chest is certain that the leopard is more deadly than the lion. Hunters tossed by the rhino and Cape buffalo insist these two animals head the "most dangerous" list. There are few men alive who have been caught up with by an elephant, but you may be sure they cast their vote for this largest of African animals. Once a man has had a brush with death because of any one particular member of the Big Five, it is hard for him to give an objective opinion.

All five animals can send a hunter to his grave if he becomes a bit careless or overconfident. And a man needs luck as well as skill when he continually exposes himself to these dangerous animals. There is a law of averages in any hazardous sport, and no one knows this better than the experienced safari hand. Also, no one is more cautious and alert than Africa's hunters—with the possible exception of Africa's Big Five. When I am asked what animal I consider most dangerous, my understating answer is the elephant. I believe most professional hunters will agree with me. Certainly the unpredictable and intelligent elephant has caused the deaths of more members of the East African Professional Hunters Association.

Some general observations can be made to begin with. The lion will conceal himself flat against the ground and can disappear into the landscape; in a thicket he is practically impossible to discern. Worse, if there is an overgrown tangle of thorns, vines, and twisted trees, he will go instinctively for the most impenetrable part and lie in wait. He has highly developed senses and knows the precise moment the charge should be made; he can run at extraordinary speed; his strength is legendary. If a man approaches past the fifteen-yard line from a lion, he is as good as dead, should the lion decide to attack. The lion springs in an enormous bound, and he is on top of the man before the hunter can raise his gun to fire. At distances farther than this, there is always another danger. Even supposing the shot is a fatal, accurate one, there is the grave danger of an animal crashing down on the man and mauling him in a last death effort.

The elephant is a peaceful animal by nature. The scent of man can cause an entire herd to leave the immediate vicinity. The elephant is a vegetarian, so he poses no threat to other animal life. Animals leave him alone—except man. An elephant could lead a peaceful existence if it were not for his coveted ivory. Therefore, man seeks the elephant and is sometimes killed for his trouble. The elephant is basically a "family-type" animal, and he resents intrusion of any type. But he will not back down one inch when he feels his person or family faces danger. The hunter will not experience bluff charges with an elephant, as he can expect with the rhino. Once an elephant spots his adversary and decides to do something about it, there is no way a man can stop his charge except with a skillfully placed frontal brain shot. Either the elephant goes down or he will wrap his powerful trunk around the hunter and smash him to death. He will use his feet and his tusks if he thinks his initial trunk assault has not caused fatal results.

The rhino will charge as many times as he runs away, and

then some of his charges are not really charges at all, but bluffs. However, when the real thing comes along, the rhino comes at you with terrifying fury. Should you be unprepared, and yet fortunate enough to escape his first charge, you may be sure others will follow. Your rifle can stop him. Nothing else will. He is a master at camouflage, rarely presenting himself in the open for an easy shot. If he knows that he is being tracked, he will lead you into the type of thick cover perfect for his murderous ambush tactics.

The leopard is the Big Five's silent messenger of death. His victims are rarely aware of his presence until instinct gives them a brief glimpse of his spotted body hurtling toward them. His weapons are his powerful jaws and cruel claws. He attacks with uncanny speed and he, too, is a master of camouflage—except occasionally, he forgets about his tail and lets it hang down from an overhead tree limb. You are fortunate if you see the spotted tail in time. You can't outrun him and few can outthink him. Once he springs upon an enemy, he will not be deterred, unless by his own death.

The Cape buffalo is crafty, devious, and unflinching in the face of continual punishment. Once committed to a charge, only death defeats him. Worse, he has an uncanny sense of what the hunter is going to do and often he is in ambush for the hunter, guessing correctly the hunter's every move. You can deflect a lion's charge, but few men have deflected a wounded buffalo's assault. By nature he is as peaceful as the domestic bull and will avoid contact with man under normal conditions. He travels in herds and is rarely disturbed by any other animal. He has taken the lives of many men who were determined to take his.

Blaney Percival, for twenty years Game Warden in British East Africa, and a famous hunter in his own right, is quoted as saying: "There are times when almost any wild animal is dangerous—when hungry, during the mating season or guarding its young; sometimes even when you disturb it in its sleep —and every now and then it will be a question of its life or yours." But Percival, like most men who have spent so much time in Africa, believed that no animal will attack a man normally without provocation. It may be, however, that a man doesn't really know when he provokes an animal.

A wounded animal is quite another story. An animal which has received a nasty shot will *almost always charge* if cornered, and may charge automatically. If you shoot any of the Big Five and do not kill the animal, be prepared for a charge. Repeat, be prepared for a charge. Naturally, every sportsman hopes and wants to bring his animal down with one shot. The fatal or effectively crippling shot is the one which renders the animal at the hunter's mercy instead of the hunter at his. But the most important thing in shooting wild game on safari is to be prepared for the shot that is not perfect. More often than not, your first shot will wound an animal instead of killing him outright. Then the trouble starts. Don't wait to see how far the animal gallops before he drops dead. Give him one or two more shots for insurance's sake. Your professional hunter will appreciate this course of action because he, not you, has to follow up the wounded animal. It is impossible for a hunter to think kindly of his client when he must track a dangerous, wounded animal through tall grass, or similar dense cover, unable to see more than a few feet in front of him, and only too conscious of the fact that somewhere around him a deadly animal lies in ambush. And all because the client wanted to be called "one-shot Jones."

Animals want to be left alone. They will not charge unless provocation is offered—yours or someone else's. There is, however, another class of animals which seems to repudiate this statement, the so-called rogues. Rogues are animals which attack a man on sight and seemingly without reason. I think a closer investigation will show the animal does have a reason for his attack.

Usually a rogue has been wounded at one time and has escaped; he has become naturally suspicious of man and his attack is motivated by a feeling of protection rather than anger. The wounded animals, whether by spears or firearms, are doubly cagey, doubly dangerous. It is likely they are still in pain from old wounds and are irascible and ready to charge at the least disturbance.

Many rogues are also castouts. When an animal becomes old and infirm and cannot keep up with his companions any longer, he either voluntarily leaves or is forceably ejected by the group. Now he faces stark survival. He must hunt on his own, but his faculties are slowed and often impaired; he has poor success. Since it is difficult to keep himself supplied with fresh meat or vegetation—depending on the game species—he remains hungry and ill-tempered. Being disturbed by a hunter doesn't brighten his disposition.

You will meet them all on safari—the Big Five and many others. I hope the ensuing chapters introduce you to these animals properly. However, the best way to know African game life is to plan a safari and meet them yourself. Then *you* can properly choose which member of the Big Five you consider most dangerous.

CHAPTER III

CHUI—
The Leopard

All the authorities speak of the leopard's strange, dry, consumptive cough; and once you hear it, you will never forget it—nor have any doubt what it means. But there is a worse thing than this warning; that is the attack in dead silence.

J. A. Hunter, one of the acknowledged greats of professional hunting, has stated that he considers the leopard Africa's most dangerous game. Hunter and his charming wife have built a comfortable hotel one hundred miles outside Nairobi on the main road leading to Mombasa, Kenya's seaport. They call the hotel Hunter's Lodge, and this is where I had a chance to chat with him about his ideas on leopard.

Hunter feels that once a leopard sights a man and is convinced the man has seen him, he will charge *whether he is wounded or not.* If *chui* feels he has not been detected, he will generally streak for cover, but occasionally a particularly treacherous leopard will lie low and wait. No one will ever know how many men have been within a hairbreadth of death as they passed under a tree, a leopard overhead crouched and waiting, safe themselves only because the leopard felt safe. Once the leopard feels he has been detected, however, he does not hesitate. He springs.

Lions give a warning growl; the leopard may emit his consumptive cough, or he may not—he can leap on his victim in awesome silence.

The lion and leopard are equally dangerous in the clawing they give a man. The animals feast on carrion and a clawing almost inevitably results in blood poisoning. But while the lion will claw with only its front paws, the leopard uses all four. A leopard's favorite trick is to disembowel his victim with the claws of his hind feet while anchoring his front paw claws into the victim's shoulders, chest and neck. In a matter of seconds, the cat can mangle a man to death.

There is one other attribute in hunting leopard that must be considered, which is not true of the other Big Five. The leopard is particularly treacherous because he can hide *above* a man. You have to keep a sharp lookout overhead as well as ahead of you when you are stalking *chui*.

The Lololunga area of Northern Masailand is excellent country for hunting leopard. The thickly wooded mountains offer the type of protective covering that leopards like best. Wart hogs and baboons, the smaller varieties of antelope, and gazelle—the leopard's favorite foods—abound; water is plentiful. But the leopard is hardly ever encountered in the open, almost never in daylight, preferring to hide by day and hunt by night, and this makes him difficult to bag. Worse, he is the most suspicious and wary of the Big Five.

The most practical way to approach leopard hunting is to make the leopard come to you. Bait is the answer. A small antelope or gazelle will do, but you will probably fare better if you tempt *chui* with his weakness, wart hog or baboon.

The wart hog is Africa's wild pig. His long upper tusks

make an interesting trophy. African wart hogs live in families and have a better disposition than other species of wild pig found throughout the world. These creatures are extremely cautious and generally remain in thick underbrush. When alarmed, they run with their tails straight up in the air, something like a danger antenna.

So let's say you have a wart hog with which to entice the leopard. Select a tree in a semiopen area, but remember, you need thick underbrush nearby in which to conceal yourself. The tree should have at least one strong limb, and it is preferable that your view should not be obscured by overlapping branches and foliage.

Let the bait get good and ripe. The higher the better. Then cut it partially open and by means of a long rope or steel cable attached to your hunting car, drag it around the countryside within a half-mile radius or more. The trick is to get the bait into thick underbrush as well as dragging it in the open. This is sometimes difficult, but hunting cars are sturdy vehicles. The purpose, of course, is to give the leopard a clue to the bait when he is on his way to water, or simply on the prowl after dark. Once the leopard picks up the scent, the first stage of your hunt is over. *Chui* will make directly for the wart hog.

Finish by hauling the bait up to the chosen tree; hang it there firmly by lashing it to the tree limb. You might run into the problem of vultures. In a matter of hours, these giant, huge-winged birds may be making a feast of your bait unless you can hide it from their sharp eyes. I have found that using leaves to cover the lure helps; the leopard can find it just as well as if it were out in the open, but the vultures won't be likely to spot it. Another way of discouraging these pesky birds is to hang strips of gauze, or any other fluttering material, around the carcass. Apparently, strange movement discourages the scavengers.

The natural blind where you are going to wait is very important. I would suggest your concealment might best be a bush anywhere from forty to eighty yards from the tree. Check the prevailing wind to be sure your blind is downwind. With a sharp *panga* (an African machete) hack out an opening and prepare an area inside the cover where you and your hunting companion can wait. Take care to clear away stones, pointed branches and dry, fallen twigs. They all make noise and a leopard blind must be deadly quiet at all times in order to fool this crafty spotted cat. It is well to take great pains with the blind. Make it comfortable. You may have to wait only a day, but then again you could spend four, five days or a week waiting for *chui* to put in an appearance.

Leave a small opening through the blind for your rifle and sufficient space for you to see the tree clearly. The essential problem is to have the blind undetectable by the leopard, but to be able to see and shoot clearly. A leopard's eyesight is so sharp that the slightest movement will arouse his suspicions and nothing will persuade him to go near your bait.

I remember my first leopard vividly. We had carefully prepared the blind, conscientiously dragged the wart hog over a mile area, and left our bait tied securely in a tree. The following day, we hunted antelope in another area and returned to our place of concealment in midafternoon to wait for *chui*. Apparently, no leopard had crossed the area where we had dragged the bait. The carcass had not been touched. The same discouraging results happened the second and third day.

On the morning of the fourth day, we discovered the bait had been chewed on sometime during the previous night. Medium-sized tracks at the foot of the tree indicated that there was either a large female or a medium-sized male dining on our wart hog.

About four o'clock that afternoon, we made our preparations. Our Land Rover driver steered us as close as possible to the blind's entrance. A hunting companion and I slipped out of the hunting car and into the undercover brush. The car kept moving at a steady pace toward more open ground. Should the leopard be nearby watching, we were sure he would give his attention to the moving vehicle and not to us. Once the car had departed, he would feel safe to come out of hiding. We settled down and my eyes never left the bait.

An hour passed, then another hour ticked by, and I began to examine my watch worriedly. It was nearly six-thirty and there was only about fifteen or twenty minutes of light left. At that moment, I tried to console myself·with the advice I had heard from the best leopard hunters in Africa: "More leopards are shot in the last half hour of light than all other times put together."

When I looked at the tree with my naked eye, instead of using my rifle scope, I could scarcely make out the bait. The branches were even more blurred. My eyes were burning with strain, but I leaned forward and resumed my vigil, peering through my four-power scope.

I should like to report that I watched the leopard make his stealthy approach to the tree and I sat in the blind holding back my excitement until the leopard presented a perfect shot. But there is a mystery about leopards that I had heard of all my hunting life and which I now had verified. Now you see him, now you don't. I know few hunters who can honestly testify that they have seen a leopard streak from nearby cover and climb the baited tree. You look at the tree through your scope and one second all you see is a bare limb and the bait;

then faster than the eye can blink, the leopard is crouched on the same limb taking a cautious last look around.

This is what had happened to me, and I was really in luck, for the animal before me was a beautiful specimen. I checked my impulse to fire. The light was very bad, and I had to be particularly careful of my shot because nothing can be worse than stalking a wounded leopard in approaching darkness. With the trophy so close, I didn't want to miss.

My leopard stretched and reached with his two powerful front paws for the wart hog. He had forgotten his earlier caution; all *chui* was thinking about was the delicious meal we had prepared for him. I raised the sight of my scope to shoulder height and aimed for the leopard's heart, squeezing the trigger.

There was a whirring motion and the leopard dropped to the ground with a thud. But I reminded myself of the hunter's first rule: Never assume your animal is dead; always assume he will get up and charge. I approached slowly and waited. Nothing happened. Then I saw my leopard sprawled under the tree limb. He was very dead.

I can think back on a couple of other episodes which really chill my blood. Once my gunbearer saw me pass directly below a big male leopard. Kamuya, wisely, gave me no cry of alarm. Only after I was a safe distance away did he signal. Happily, the leopard was now far enough away to feel he was not trapped; had I looked up and seen him, he would have leaped without a second's hesitation and his closeness, my surprise, and the leopard's speed would surely have resulted in a most unpleasant meeting.

Another time our safari party had been hunting leopard for almost a month, without any success. There were leopards around, but they were exceedingly wary, and refused to come out before dark. (To hunt animals at night with flashlights, lamps, or such, as some of the earlier hunters did, has long been outlawed. An exception is made for man-eating animals or animals which are doing an excessive amount of damage to field crops, or which have taken to killing livestock. In such cases, game wardens sometimes dispatch the troublemakers at night, using powerful light beams to search out these animals. The light momentarily blinds the animal intruders, thus permitting a perfect shot.)

A total of six baits had been hung and still there was not a chance of firing, although a check in the mornings showed that four had been chewed upon. This meant there were four leopards within a mile of the camp. Every night back at camp we heard the leopards' sawing coughs. We began to wonder if those leopards weren't enjoying their private joke on us.

Early the next morning, I sent my best tracker, Masyoka, to find out which bait, if any, had been disturbed. He reported within the hour that a bait no more than three-quarters of a mile away had been touched. The tracks were those of a big male. He had not eaten much, which led me to believe he had not come upon this particular bait until early morning. That meant he was still hungry and there was a good chance he would not wait for total darkness to continue the feast.

At noon we drove over to the bait. No one got out. Everyone felt sure we had arrived early enough to fool the leopard, who was probably several miles away, but we decided not to take any chances. We drove as close to the blind as possible, jumped out as the vehicle was moving, and made our silent bid for cover. Three of us quickly slipped through the small passageway and into the semidarkness of our leopard blind. An instant later, we heard a cough, a deep, low growl. I saw a

flash of yellow, and then four forms emerged from the blind—
the three of us and the leopard.

I don't know who was more shocked and surprised, *chui*
or us, but I am happy to say the leopard turned tail and ran.
Often with leopards, the luck is not so auspicious. One
of the greatest hunters in the world, Eric Rungren, tells
of a time his luck almost ran out. A client of Eric's had made
a hurried shot against the professional hunter's advice. The
shot wounded the animal, but did not stop him; the next
moment he was upon Eric. Rungren is one of the few men I
have ever heard of who literally choked a leopard to death.
(Carl Ackerley, the noted explorer, is another.) Eric has scars
all over his body to show for his experience. But he is lucky
to be alive. In battles between men and leopards, man makes
a much poorer showing that the animal.

Large leopards measure over eight feet, weight up to one
hundred sixty pounds. Their speed, their agility, and their
tremendous force make them more than a match for even
giants among men.

A leopard who turns into a man-eater or a man-mauler is
more deadly and dangerous than the lion of the same procliv-
ities. Leopards seem to lose all fear when they turn on humans;
they will lie in wait on an overhead branch, watching the
movements of a village, knowing that sooner or later a trip
to the water supply or the fields surrounding the village will
give them their chance. Silent, cunning, sly, they wait for the
straggler and spring on the victim before a cry has escaped
his lips.

John Taylor, in his book *Pondoro, Last of the Ivory
Hunters*, tells of a man-eater who so terrified an entire area
that everyone, with the exception of two families, fled the

district. Ominously, he never records what happened to those who elected to stay.

Taylor insists that the size of the leopard is what makes it seem less dangerous than the lion, that if the two were matched in size and weight, he has no doubt the leopard would be much more ferocious. "They are much bolder than the lion at night," he writes; "human habitations hold no terrors for them. They will enter a house through an open door or window and prowl right through it—not excepting the room in which you're sleeping—in the hope of finding a dog, which the leopard prefers to all other food. But if he is not a man-eater, the leopard won't touch you even though he is in the same room with you—you won't know of his visit until the next morning." I, for one, do not want to prove or disprove Mr. Taylor's theory. If I ever have a leopard visit the private confines of my sleeping area (and I happen to wake up), I shall be a rather rude host and evacuate my quarters immediately. I only trust that I do not resemble either a dog or man in flight.

Not all authorities agree with Taylor that dog is the leopard's favorite repast; a great many hunters, myself included, would state baboon. When I first visited Africa, it seemed to me that baboons were a little too human to hunt. However, after a certain amount of experience, I found that the baboon was not the harmless, lovable animal I had first imagined. Baboons are vicious and tricky; they have been known to attack villages in numbers and drag off small children and kill them. While a single baboon seldom attacks men and women, there are recorded incidents in which groups have gone for settlers. Baboons have great strength in their long, powerful arms and they will bite, claw, and strangle their victims.

Once a group, or colony, of baboons attacked two white settlers on their farm. African field laborers witnessed the incident (after they locked themselves in a work shed) but were too afraid to help their "white *bwanas*." The settlers were plowing land at the forest's edge when they were ambushed by these snarling baboons. The two farmers were able to shoot nine baboons and seven more were mortally wounded with crushed skulls. Both men were fighting a losing battle once they had emptied their rifles, but they continued to defend themselves by swinging their weapons at the snapping attackers. Unfortunately, there were too many baboons and both farmers met a most unpleasant death. This story re-emphasizes that no African animal should be underestimated by the safari client, regardless of size and comical appearance. In the main, however, the Africans' case against the baboon is that he destroys crops, raids fields, and ruins gardens. For myself, I have another grievance. On a number of occasions, I have been stalking a particular trophy for hours only to have the baboon screech out a warning just as I had the animal lined up in my rifle sight. My personal nickname for baboon is "blabbermouth" for just this reason.

The best weapon against the leopard, in my opinion, is the .300 Magnum or the .375. The chances are your professional hunter will choose a second weapon for your use, either a double-barreled heavy-caliber rifle or a shotgun in case you do not wound your animal on your first shot. Some leopards attack the instant they hear a shot fired, and professionals feel a shotgun's blast offers better protection and less chance of missing the target than most rifles. A bolt-action rifle is no good at all, particularly in dense cover where you can be ambushed and not even have sufficient time to raise your weapon to your shoulder. If you do not have a shotgun, a double-barreled heavy-caliber rifle is almost as efficient at close quarters.

I'd like to finish up the stories of the leopard with an experience Teddy Roosevelt and son Kermit had when they were in British East Africa. The trackers had sighted a leopard and were in the process of driving it toward the Roosevelt party when the leopard—without warning—charged Roosevelt's son. Kermit, who was not yet twenty, showed his instinctive hunting skill. He stood still, fired, and stopped the leopard's first charge a scant six yards away from him. The leopard then turned and Kermit fired again, crippling him.

Roosevelt remarks, "The wounds were fatal, and they would have knocked the fight out of any animal less plucky and savage than the leopard; but, not even in Africa, is there a beast of more unflinching courage than this spotted cat. The beaters were much excited by the charge and one of them . . . went too near it, and out came the wounded leopard at him. It was badly crippled or it would have got the beater at once. As it was, it was slowly overtaking him as he ran through the tall grass when McMillan [another member of the party] standing on an antheap, shot it again. Yet, in spite of having this third bullet in it, it ran down the beater and seized him, worrying him with teeth and claws. It was weak because of its wounds, and the powerful savage wrenched himself free, while McMillan fired into the beast again, and back it went through the long grass into the thicket. There was a pause, and the wounded beater was removed to a place of safety, while a messenger was sent on to us to bring up the Boer dogs. But while they were waiting, the leopard, on its own initiative, came again straight at Kermit, and this time it dropped dead at Kermit's bullet. No animal could have shown a more fearless and resolute temper. It was an old female, but small, its weight being a little short of seventy pounds."

Chui is a fine trophy and certainly well worth the time and trouble it necessarily takes to shoot one. Stay alert at all times. The leopard is most particular about the company he keeps and I can promise you he will not wait around long enough to enjoy yours if you become careless during the hunt. One final word. The leopard knows only two ways to run. In case you do not see his spotted tail streaking off in the opposite direction, you are apt to be looking down his snarling throat.

CHAPTER **IV**

SIMBA
The Lion

Lions, unlike leopards, travel in groups and have a strong feeling for family. These groups, which may be as large as twenty or thirty, but more often number ten or fifteen, are called prides.

Most of the kills are made by the female lion although it is not unusual for two young males or a young male and female to pair up when they hunt. Zebras are perhaps the lion's favorite food and their distinctive marking makes them easily detectable. The lion crawls on his belly downwind toward a herd of zebras, camouflaging himself in long grasses or behind small scrub. Should a zebra happen to glance in his direction, the lion immediately freezes. While the lion is crawling into a position of attack, other lions from the pride join the hunt, circling the herd. One remaining lion shows himself at the far end of the circle and springs the trap. The zebras panic and scatter—toward the carefully concealed and waiting lions.

There are some lions which lack courage and are most careful about what game species they attack for food. Lions have had their skulls fractured by the powerful kick of a mother giraffe protecting her young. The eland's powerful spiral horns have been known to disembowel *simba*. The greater kudu and sable antelope have left formidable scars on lion hides, and lions stay away completely from the rhino, Cape buffalo and elephant.

Lions show bursts of speed only for short distances. They will give up the chase if outsmarted or outrun. I have even seen the stupid wildebeest outthink and outrun a lion, the same thing being true with the zebra, kongoni, oryx, topi, ostrich and even the wart hog. Should a lion be made a fool of and miss his target, he will stalk off with false pride, ignoring the clouds of dust left from the stampeding animals. The lion is suffering from "hurt feelings" and it is rather a comical scene to witness.

An animal's sixth sense is often mentioned around safari campfires. It reminds me of the strange situation which exists in Africa between lions and plains-game animals. Plains-game animals must have a sixth sense or "special feeling," for they know when lions are hungry. They can spot a lion hundreds of feet away and "feel" the mood of their natural enemy. If the lion is hungry, a silent message spreads like wildfire and the plains game gallop off. At other times you will see lions among antelope, zebra, gazelle, and giraffe. The plains-game animals ignore the lions, for their sixth sense tells them that they are not in danger. These same animals will even drink alongside lions at a water hole—truly one of Africa's strangest spectacles.

People are always interested in hearing about man-eaters. I, for one, believe many of these man-eating tales are grossly exaggerated. Only in rare instances do lions purposely kill humans for food.

In most cases reported, authorities found that sick or

wounded lions have become man-eaters. Man is easier to attack than a swift, alert antelope or zebra. But once *simba* tastes human flesh, he has the unfortunate habit of foregoing other gastronomic pleasures.

Africans themselves have been the principal ones responsible for the majority of man-eating lions. Many tribes have a most unchristian habit of leaving their dead or dying out in the plains to be disposed of by Africa's scavengers—the hyena, buzzard, jackal, wild dog, and stork. This primitive custom causes these same tribesmen eventual grief from lions. Instead of a scavenger finding the tribal outcasts and dead first, a lion comes along and finds a ready-made meal for himself. Shortly thereafter, *simba* decides to feast on a very much alive villager. Now the village lives in a state of terror because of the man-eater in the area. Authorities have continually warned tribes about this backward practice, but it takes a long, long time to change African custom.

The recent death of two Africans, caused by man-eating lions, points out just how clever and fast man-eaters can be, once they become killers. A district officer was driving on the road between Nairobi and Voi National Park. He passed two tribesmen whom he recognized as relatives of a local tribal chief. The district officer continued on for approximately three minutes and then decided to turn back so he could have a word with the tribesmen. He had meant to give the two Africans a message for their chief, and was slightly perplexed when he could not find a trace of the Africans. At the time, he reasoned they might have gotten a lift, although he could not remember any vehicles passing him on the road. The government official forgot about the incident until later that afternoon when he received an urgent phone call from an assistant, reporting that two badly chewed up bodies had been found in the district. The district officer drove immediately to the scene and found, to his horror, the mauled bodies of the two tribesmen he had passed earlier that day. They were the victims of a pair of man-eating lions. The drag marks and tracks told the story. The man-eaters had attacked the tribesmen while they were still on the road and dragged them just thirty yards off the roadside before proceeding with their meal. All of this took place during the eight-minute period when the district officer first saw the tribesmen and returned to give them the message. In fact, the lions must have been crouched in the flats while the district officer made several runs up and down the road in search of the Africans.

The elephant usually trumpets before a charge; the rhino grunts and kicks up dust. The Cape buffalo snorts and emits a throaty bellow; the lion gives a resonant growl and springs. A man on the receiving end of a charge of an animal with five hundred pounds of snarling determination has no other choice but to stand ground, fire, and hope his shots were true. No matter what the instinct, NEVER RUN. It is absolutely impossible to outrun a lion (or for that matter, any wild game animal), which has twice the speed of a man and a hundred times the determination. Tall tales have been told about men who ran, climbed trees, and thus escaped a lion's fury. I would put no trust in such a refuge. Lions can reach remarkably far—sixteen feet has often been reported—and although there is the well-known theory lions can't climb trees, I have seen lions do so.

Sir Alfred Pease has a rule that there should never be less than two hundred yards between a lion and himself. He was always reminding his hunting companions that this was one of his favorite maxims of the way to avoid danger; but one day Pease was out hunting with a friend who thought him overly conservative and, chasing an animal which had been hurt, went within a hundred yards of the wounded animal. The lion charged and, although Pease fired shot after shot into it, he was not able to stop it until it had clawed his friend so badly that he died soon afterward.

I do not wish to take exception with Sir Alfred. Nevertheless, I am not an advocate of long-range shooting. My personal experience tells me that any hunter, experienced or not, is more likely to wound an animal at so great a distance, especially if one doesn't have a clear shot at the animal. The closer one can approach any dangerous game animal (within reason, of course), the more assured he can be of an instantaneous kill. It stands to reason that the animal's "fatal areas" are that much easier to hit.

The best place to aim is either the head or the center of the shoulder. (If you take a hind shot, presuming that a friend is the one being attacked, shoot for the base of the tail and hope to sever the spine.) Édouard Foa, the French hunter, insisted that the perfect shot for lions was in the neck. He used a .303 rifle and maintained that with this gun there were two advantages to the neck shot: If the shot was true, the spine severed and the animal dropped dead; if the shot missed its mark, it passed directly through the neck without seriously wounding the animal. I myself would consider a lion wounded in the neck a most vicious and determined adversary.

The terrible danger of a wounded lion lies in the fact that it can have its heart blown to shreds and still continue to charge. Lions with vital organs shot away have been known to continue their charge until they toppled a man and either badly mauled or killed him. I might add that a disclosure of facts revealed the hunter used too light a gun caliber in such cases. One of the worst aspects of a mauling by a lion, like that by a leopard, is the danger of infection. The leopard and lion claws are hollow and rotten meat is sure to be lodged in the talons. Gangrene infection has claimed many lives, particularly in the past when there was no way to get a wounded man to a doctor save carrying him in a sling over miles and miles of rough, uninhabited country. In the meantime, the wound festered and became infected. Even an amputation was often too late.

Although in the old days lions could be bagged almost outside Nairobi, it is no disgrace nowadays for a forty-five-day safari to come back without one good-maned trophy. You are bound to see elephant, Cape buffalo, rhino, and perhaps leopard, but it requires a combination of hunting skill and *luck* to see a mature maned lion.

The Game Department realizes the danger and protects the remaining lions by insisting that sportsmen and settlers buy a special license that permits only one male per hunter.

There are other reasons why the lion has decreased besides the inroads made by hunters and the early wanton slaughter by some of the first settlers. Lions are found near plains because the animals they prefer as food—zebra, ostrich, giraffe, antelope, and gazelle—inhabit these areas. When you find this type of open land, you will also, quite naturally, find native settlements, since it is easier to cultivate crops in an area already cleared than to have to clear it.

Africans have been taught the simple methods of farming by European administration; and as a result, the natives have pushed farther and farther into areas formerly considered lion territory. Not only have the presence of natives in their fields tended to discourage the lion from frequenting old haunts, but the presence of livestock was a temptation which often led him into serious trouble. Repeated attacks on livestock in the beginning had to be stopped. The natives organized and systematically hunted out lions and killed them off. This was aided and abetted by the settlers, and for many years there was indiscriminate killing.

The Masai are Africa's greatest cattle raisers. They live completely on the blood and milk of their cattle, refusing any other types of food. It is natural that these natives come in contact with lions more than any of their fellow tribes because the cattle they raise are a natural target for *simba*. The lion is the Masai's sworn enemy and the greatest feat of a Masai warrior is to "bloody his spear" by attacking a lion.

The Masai used to have a regular ritual in killing lions. Once a lion had been spotted, the warriors formed a solid ring around the animal. As the circle became smaller the lion would charge, trying to escape. The African that the lion attacked considered the charge a great honor and stood with his spear and shield against the oncoming beast. As the lion leapt on his victim, the other Masai jumped into the battle, trying to spear *simba* to death. The only trouble was that too often the original warrior the lion attacked was killed and many of the other Africans were badly mauled, or got in the way of a carelessly thrust spear.

Officially, this form of "hunting" no longer exists, but the young warriors of the Masai nation still have their private ceremonies, much to the chagrin of game conservation officials. Game wardens have recently warned the Masai nation that harsher steps will be taken if the tribes refuse to stop hunting lions, but it is hard for the wardens to make the ideas of game preservation as meaningful as generations of ritual.

Nevertheless, the Masailand is the greatest area left for lion hunting in British East Africa. A good way to get your lawful lion is, like the method employed for the leopard, to set a trap by dragging a dead piece of bait, preferably zebra or antelope, in a circle. You drag the bait over a considerable area and then string it up, hoping the lion catches the scent and follows it to the bait. One would think that seeing a zebra hanging from a tree would arouse the lion's suspicions. After all, lions have grown up hunting zebra and watching their habits, and certainly should be able to reason that zebras do not inhabit trees like monkeys. No such thing is the case; perhaps hunger has something to do with their avidity, but whatever the reason, I have never known a lion to show any reluctance to go directly to a hamstrung zebra.

One problem no hunter has been able to solve is keeping the hyena away from the bait. Usually a leopard bait is hung in the tree too high for the hyena, but the larger lion bait is another matter. Then the scavengers are able to stand on their hind quarters and feast on the hind quarters of the bait.

When approaching a blind, I have often heard their snapping steel-like jaws, and I could hardly contain my anger. Generally speaking, when hyenas are at the bait lions are not in the area, though this is not always the case. Hyenas are cowardly creatures and move off at the first indication of another animal approaching, but occasionally they will hang about while a lion is feasting, careful to keep out of sight, but knowing that when *simba* leaves they can return to the remains.

Many lions have been shot who could not stand the idea of hyenas sharing their bait, even though these same lions knew it unwise to show themselves before dark. Hunters have reported shooting beautiful trophies quite by accident when they saw a lion come out charging at the hyenas.

The blind that is so useful for shooting leopard is also an excellent device for bagging a lion. However, safari members must be careful how they acquire their place of concealment. Game laws specifically state a lion blind must be natural and untampered with. This means that one cannot "build" a blind. A few branches and other types of foliage may be gathered to perfect concealment, but the chosen thicket, bush, etc., cannot be sliced up and permanently damaged. The law is less stringent on leopard blinds.

Concealed in the lion blind, you wait at dawn and dusk. Although the method of hunting lions is practically the same as hunting leopards, there is an additional chance of finding the lions at the bait in the early hours of the morning. Lions feed during the first light of day, but as the sun comes up they take to cover. This is particularly true since more Africans have moved their villages into lion country. Lions know that villagers take their herds out to graze, that safari parties are on the move, and that groups of natives are wandering around the countryside visiting other villages. Therefore, just as the last half hour before dark is the best time to find a leopard, so the first half hour of morning light is the best time for hunting a lion. However, many lions have been shot in late afternoon, once the countryside is void of human activity and *simba* feels it safe to begin an early supper.

It would take volumes to tell all the lion stories that have come out of Africa, but every hunter has his favorite from which he cannot be dissuaded, and here is mine.

We had been hunting lions without success for over a month and a half. We had booked, in advance with the Game Department, a section of the finest lion area left in Africa, the Narok controlled-hunting area in Kenya. (Only so many safaris are allowed each year, and there are strict regulations on the number of lions that can be shot.)

There is no question that this is lion country; the circle of huts in the *bomas*, or villages, is surrounded by a wall of thick thorn tree branches in the hope that the sharp thorns will stop a lion from visiting the villagers at night. The Masai build their huts in a complete circle leaving the center space for their cattle to rest in at night.

When we visited the local Masai *bomas* in order to find out the latest lion news, all had the same story to report. Yes, they had seen and heard lions—big ones with bushy manes. They were eager to have us in the area, for our guns would be protection for their cattle and themselves against lion raids.

After you hunt a while in Africa, you learn to take some of the stories with a grain of salt. You cannot really blame the Africans for exaggerating if they can protect cattle and human life, but sometimes these tall tales can waste a lot of time. However, one story did not sound too farfetched. A pride of lions had been hunting near a chief's *boma*. The lions had killed a cow at least once every three days, and this had been going on for nearly three weeks. Apparently, the pride had no fear of the Masai herdsmen. The lions had openly attacked the cattle in broad daylight, and had given chase to one herdsman. We checked where the lion kills had been made and found the bones of the cattle. The unfortunate native was still shaking with fright. That night, we heard the roar of the lions calling to each other in the hills close by.

We picked a spot for our blind, not too far off from the *boma*, but still in dense enough cover so we felt the lions would feed without feeling disturbed. There was a perfect tree for hanging bait and natural cover nearby, a thick clump of underbrush growing next to a rock ledge.

The next day I shot a zebra and an ostrich, two favorite foods of *simba*. We dragged the carcasses for a mile near where we had heard the lions roaring the night before and finally hung the bait in the tree I had selected.

That evening we slept in the *boma* so that there would be no chance of the lions being scared off by headlights or the sound of the Land Rover engine. The Masai villagers were excited and nervous and their chattering throughout the night did not give our party much chance to sleep.

We started out at three o'clock the next morning. We knew we needed those two hours to grope our way in the darkness to our blind. We had marked the way the day before with a path of leaves leading from the *boma* to our lion blind. There was no question, as we inched nearer the blind, that lions were feeding at the bait; we could hear their grunts and the crackling of bones. I was conscious of the terrible pounding of my heart and certain that the noise would give our position away.

Fifty yards ahead was our entranceway, between the rock ledge and the thicket. It was still dark and we could not see very much, but we could tell from the snarls that the big cats were fighting over their share of the bait. From the sounds, we estimated there were at least five lions.

One of the Masai warriors, who had volunteered to help us, brushed into something he thought to be a lion. He let out a war whoop and made the one-hundred-yard dash about as fast as I have ever seen. What actually happened was that his bare leg touched one of the local tame dogs from the village who had decided to come along for the morning walk. (I am sure if the dog had known the purpose of our journey, he would have stayed home with the rest of his canine friends.) Apparently the dog thought the whole thing was a game of some type and went barking merrily after the peculiar African, who was waving his arms as he ran back toward the *boma*. I had no idea how the lions felt, but I knew from their roaring they were seriously talking over the situation. It left us in a most awkward position, because it was still too dark to see anything clearly, and I had no desire to be run over by a pride of panicked lions. Those of us who had rifles immediately threw off our safeties. We quietly waited and hoped we would not be charged.

The first sunrays took fifteen minutes to filter through the night's shadows, although it seemed to me like hours. The roars were farther off now and we were thankful that the pride retained its natural sense of caution. I might add, that particular Masai tracker who let out the whoop was read the riot act all day by the village elders.

Roy Homme, one of the all-time great hunters, and I decided we would go back to our blind later that morning and cut down the bait. This was good hunting manners and, besides, rope is too valuable a piece of equipment to throw away.

Our safari boys were packing our camp gear into the truck, and the rest of the party remained at the *boma* to take some final pictures of the Masai.

I can clearly recall Roy and me laughing and chattering about some former nonsensical hunting experience. We went into the blind to make sure nothing had dropped out of our pockets earlier; and I was in the midst of telling Roy something, when the surprised and horrified expression on his face made me stop my words in midsentence. I followed his stare and there, completely surrounding us, was a pride of lions— old and young males, lionesses with cubs; in short, the whole family. Automatically we checked the wind.

A sharp plains breeze had come up and the force of this wind not only protected our scent, but had kept our voices from carrying. As if in slow motion, we lowered ourselves to the ground. Silently we crawled into our cover. One male with a fine-looking tawny mane was a trophy that would have been especially fine for the collection of African animals I was in the process of shooting for a museum. As luck would have it, this big male was feeding directly behind the tree and offered an almost impossible shot. Fair enough, I would wait.

Neither Roy nor I had gotten over our astonishment at finding lions stretched out contentedly in the midday sun, unconcerned with the distant shouts of natives herding their cattle in the hills. We did not know at the time if this was the same pride we had recently encountered. As it turned out, the pride we faced was an entirely different lion group which had probably just entered the area.

Roy and I settled back in a comfortable shooting position. All we had to do now was pray a wind change did not give away our position. Then I really got the shock of my life. I felt what seemed like a thousand needles pricking the entire lower part of my body. Then Roy started squirming and bit his own hand to keep silent because of the immediate danger all around us. We had not been careful to check the ground before we lay down. We had chosen the spot on which a stream of literally thousands of safu ants had decided to gather. Each one of these little devils has pincerlike jaws. They will bite through clothing, so you can imagine the effect they have on bare flesh. We had to get them off us and yet we had to use the utmost caution, for there were eleven lions munching zebra bones less than fifteen yards away. I cannot think when I have gotten out of part of my clothing so fast (that is, in the bush). We finally managed to get the ants off, but our bodies were a mass of stinging bites.

Several times some of the lions looked in our direction, and one lioness in particular seemed to sense something was not quite right. We moved our position as far away from the ants as possible, and resumed our wait.

Suddenly the lioness stood up, sniffing the air in our direction. Slowly, very slowly, she approached our hiding place. I certainly didn't want to shoot the lioness—particularly after I had seen the fine male—and also there would be a great deal of embarrassing explanation due the Game Department.

The lioness stopped about twelve feet from us and lay down. She must have had a better view from her prone position, for immediately she let loose a series of low, throaty growls. The other lions were all immediately on guard. Now five or six looked in our direction.

The lioness sprang to her feet and started to approach the blind, her growls louder and more menacing. I had forgotten all about the Game Department and was all set to shoot. The lioness' eyes never left mine, and I can remember thinking how beautiful and yet frightening they were—yellow pools of anger. Her tail twitched once, twice—and I knew that the third time she would be in mid-air, ripping and clawing her way on top of us.

As she let out one final roar, four feet away, I snapped my rifle to my shoulder and fired blindly into her gaping jaws. Roy, who has hunted lions all his life, told me another second and neither one of us would have left the blind alive. My shot caught her in the mouth and she somersaulted backwards. The rest of the pride were on their feet, some growling in our direction, others hurrying over to their mortally wounded companion.

Roy and I beat a hasty retreat out of the blind, for now that we had been discovered, we would have a better chance against ten lions if we were out in the open. Then we got another shock. There were not ten lions. There were sixteen in all. Where the other six came from, I shall never know.

A young male and a lioness padded silently toward us in a half-crouching position. Roy purposely shot directly in front of them, his bullet throwing dirt up in their faces. This stopped them for a moment.

I fired two shots over the heads of the nearest group of five lions, expecting the entire pride to turn and run for cover. Two of the lions answered my shots with angry roars. They did not charge, but they did not retreat.

Now the lions appeared to be grouping. We loaded our rifles to full capacity, not caring any more about the noise the metallic click of our bolts made. So far, neither Roy nor I had spoken; we were not quite sure what the effect of the sound of our voices would be.

Then I heard the most beautiful noise in my life: the sound of our Land Rover racing toward our position, horn blowing, safari crew shouting. The driver wisely headed the hunting car between the lions and us. Now I was sure the lions would give ground. But I was mistaken. Not one of them bolted. All the lions were roaring their defiance, and some of them started for the Land Rover menacingly.

The back of the Land Rover was filled with our trackers, gunbearers, and four Masai warriors brandishing their spears. And while this was somewhat reassuring, it was also inconvenient, because there was no room in the back for us. So Roy and I discreetly retired behind the Land Rover.

Now six rifles and four spears were trained on the lions as Roy and I crouched behind the car. All of us were shouting, some of us were waving our hats, the driver was blowing the horn, rifles exploded, the motor was racing. It sounded like a Fourth of July celebration.

As if by silent command, the pride turned and walked—not ran—away. One or two of them paused and, turning, gave us contemptuous looks.

We had a lot of explaining to do about that lioness and we got some funny looks, but we were at least able to sit on the veranda of the Norfolk Hotel later and *talk* about it. Roy and I were convinced of one thing—you never know what a lion is going to do next.

Anyone who has hunted Africa must have gone on at least one wild-goose chase because of a youngster's imagination. So when one day an African boy reported he had just seen a black-maned lion less than a half hour before, I did not become overly excited. The youngster was obviously disturbed with my attitude, but he kept insisting that I accompany him and see for myself if he was not telling the truth. I agreed to go because I knew he would be pestering me all day. We were approaching the fringe of a thicket when the boy stopped suddenly and pointed toward a clump of tall bushes only a few yards away. He proudly announced that *simba* was resting somewhere in those bushes. I looked at him and became furious, for now I was certain the youngster had lied to me. No one, including myself, armed with a heavy-caliber rifle, would approach a lion at so close a distance, and especially with such a carefree attitude. My angry face must have told the boy that I thought I had been tricked. He grabbed a long stick and motioned me to follow, all the time insisting, "*Simba* there, *Bwana*." I was about to call a halt to this little game when there was a tremendous roar, and the thicket seemed to leap to life. A black-maned lion jumped up practically stiff-legged and disappeared farther into the forest.

I need not say how ashamed I felt. I shook my young

guide's hand and departed, but not before I presented him with my hunting knife.

My favorite story about a lion, however, does not concern the shooting of one, rather the saving of one.

George Adamson, one of British East Africa's finest game rangers, is in charge of Kenya's wild Northern Frontier District. Several years ago, he went out in search of one lion and two lionesses that had killed a Masai tribesman. He was camped at Melka Loni, a site on a dry sandy river bed. George was in the process of tracking the trio when one of the lionesses charged and he killed her. As he was bending over the body, he heard the mewing of cubs and discovered, in a nearby rock, three female lion cubs four days old. The cubs would starve if he left them and he didn't want to destroy them. There seemed no choice but to take them back to camp at Melka Loni. There his wife, Joy, took command and gave the cubs diluted, unsweetened canned milk on which they thrived.

The youngest, the runt, was named Elsa after a friend of Joy's, and from the first, Elsa became a favorite, and like so many runts, the pluckiest.

The cubs went instinctively in search of sand outside the tent, seemingly housebroken without a bit of difficulty. In their infancy they were very much like domestic cats, showing their affection by licking hands and feet with their rough sandpapery tongues. When the Adamsons returned home to Isiolo, the cubs went with them. By now their diet had expanded to bone meal, milk, glucose, cod liver oil, and salt. Playtime was a daily ritual and Elsa began to learn to retrieve rubber balls, to play a tug of war with an old inner tube and to "stalk" the Adamsons. Tree climbing was another of Elsa's pastimes.

By now the cubs were three months old and their teeth developed enough to consume meat. Joy Adamson imitated the regurgitation that a lioness goes through for her cubs by giving them raw mincemeat. Elsa, the runt, always seemed on the losing end, so Joy kept tasty tidbits for her and Elsa would sit in Joy's lap and show her appreciation by sucking Joy's thumb.

When the cubs were five months old, trouble started. They began to make mad rushes at donkeys and pack mules and it became increasingly apparent the trio could not be kept as pets.

By now, Joy Adamson had become so deeply attached to Elsa that she made an important decision. She decided not to give up Elsa, but to send the two larger cubs to the famous Rotterdam-Blijdrop zoo in Holland. Meanwhile, Elsa grew up to be a very fine lioness except she thought she was a human, and not a lioness at all.

George Adamson's job requires that he and his wife go on safari much of the year. Soon Elsa became a veteran traveler. Her favorite resting place was the soft bedrolls piled in the back of the Adamsons' Land Rover, where she was perfectly behaved, but must have presented a startling apparition to the occasional passer-by.

On the first safari with Elsa, a pride of lions approached the camp, and their growls and roars echoed over the hillside. Elsa stopped gnawing her bone for a moment, then shook her head and went back to munching, completely unconcerned about her own kind a few hundred yards away.

George Adamson had to shoot game in order to satisfy Elsa's hungry appetite. Elsa did not know how to kill a rabbit, and she couldn't have cared less.

She loved to chase anything that moved, a favorite game

of hers; but chasing moving things was merely a game. She would leave the Adamsons' camp daily and roam freely among herds of giraffes, antelopes, and zebras, her supposed natural enemies. Elsa merely wanted company.

After the lioness was two years old, it became obvious that she was approaching womanhood. She was increasingly restless and would wander off in the forest, sometimes not returning for twenty-four hours or so. She still followed the Adamsons on their daily walks, but she seemed constantly on the alert, listening and looking intently about her all the time.

One night there was a terrible commotion and the Adamsons heard Elsa's voice among the howls and growls of a pride of lions. When they hurried out of their tent, they saw Elsa in full moonlight between the pride and the camp. They called softly, the lions growled, Elsa wavered between the two. At last Elsa returned; but the next day she disappeared and did not return for several days.

The Adamsons were now thoroughly alarmed. Their camp was in an area much frequented by hunters on safari, and they were afraid that one of Elsa's love quests might end in her being mistaken for a normal lion, and shot.

They finally made their decision. They knew one area devoid of inhabitants where there was a particularly handsome pride. They drove Elsa the three hundred miles with dark misgivings, but there seemed nothing else to do. They were not convinced she could survive in the wilderness since, to their knowledge, she had never killed. On the trip, however, Elsa learned—and it seemed quite by accident. George had wounded a water buck and as it struggled to get away, Elsa, without warning, leapt on the struggling animal, killing it instantly. In a few days George repeated the experiment and Elsa again made the kill. In two weeks, Elsa was stalking her

William D. Holmes

The Camp Site

Wakamba Tribesmen

Wakamba Tribesmen

The Trusty Land-Rover

Dragging the Bait

The Lure

The Kill

A Prize Bull Elephant

African Water
Buck

The King
of Beasts

Rewards of the Hunt

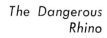

The Dangerous
Rhino

The author, with the celebrated lioness, Elsa.

own supper. At no time did this new sensation of killing animals change the lioness' feelings toward the Adamsons and their camp visitors. She was still the lovable Elsa.

The week in camp, the Adamsons played with Elsa during the day and watched while she went off at night to join the waiting pride of lions. On the seventh day, the Adamsons felt they could confidently make the final break.

Six months later, I had the pleasure of meeting Elsa. I had heard the Adamsons were going to return to the Tana River area and I asked George if I might not visit them and see the outcome of the experiment.

When I arrived, Joy gave me a list of rules that I was to follow to the letter. She cautioned me not to turn my back on Elsa; although I was assured Elsa would not leap on me in anger, the lioness might still remember her favorite game of stalking. I was also candidly asked by George if I was afraid and I said, well, he could call it apprehension. He said animals know when people are afraid and if I were really upset, Elsa would feel she was not among friends. That upset me all the more.

I assured them there was no need to worry about that, since I wasn't sure I could even get out of the canvas camp chair. They also advised me not to make any sudden movement.

Joy went down to the river where Elsa was taking a nap and the next thing I knew, the lioness came charging up the hill and directly at me. I said a small prayer that Elsa did not think I looked like an antelope. Apparently I did not, for the lioness bounded over and rubbed herself along my legs. She emitted a deep-throated purring sound, and I answered with a sigh of relief. We spent the rest of the day playing with Elsa.

Later that afternoon, I was about to leave the Adamsons' camp when I remembered the present I had brought for Elsa, a large antelope haunch in the back of the Land Rover. I offered to leave it with the Adamsons, but they told me to give it to Elsa myself. George gave me a reassuring pat, and I started off for the river carrying sixty pounds of raw meat and feeling like a damned fool. I remember calling Elsa's name extremely loudly and proceeding very slowly. On my fifth shout, I felt a stern nudge at the back of my legs. Elsa had been following me the whole time.

A recent letter from the Adamsons informs me they are proud godparents of three healthy cubs and Elsa is doing well; they plan to have family reunions when they visit their Tana River camp.

A final word about Elsa. Members of the East African Professional Hunters Association know the approximate whereabouts of Elsa. As a result, some safari clients must think it strange that they take a certain forty-mile detour when they hunt the Northern Frontier District.

CHAPTER V

TEMBO—
The Elephant

Many hunters do not agree that the lion is the king of the beasts. I happen to share their view. This does not mean the lion does not show extraordinary courage at times, but the word "king" means something very special. I think there is only one animal in Africa worthy of that name and this is the African elephant.

If the question were asked of professional hunters, "Which animal do you feel is the greatest challenge to hunt?" I believe the vast majority would reply, "The elephant." The African elephant is the largest of Africa's animals and in my opinion the smartest. Actually more experienced hunters, whether professionals or white settlers in Africa, have been killed by the elephant than any other member of the Big Five. I stress the word "experienced" because it makes a great difference to this statement. Probably the African Cape buffalo and rhino have killed more men, but not as many experienced hunters.

An angry rhino will try to ram his horns through you, and yet concentrated fire power will deter the animal's charge. A few men have, in single combat, killed leopards, and many have managed to absorb the leopard's mauling until a companion's shot killed the spotted cat. The Cape buffalo has tossed men and left their bodies, provided the victims have kept a cool head and remained still; men have been able to protect themselves from the lion's jaws for the few important moments it took for their rescuers to kill the animal. There are many cases on record where members of a hunting party have distracted the attention of all four of these animals and saved a hunter from a second charge, but an army could not distract an elephant's attention once you are in his grasp.

Cases of men being caught by elephants and escaping, even with serious wounds, are rare. Stories are often told of men (mostly Africans) running *underneath* an elephant and dodging about the legs and thus avoiding death. Elephants have poor sight and in a densely thicketed forest often find it impossible to distinguish a man from the shadows and play of light. At any rate, here is one hunter who hopes he never has to rely on such fancy footwork. I have been up to within twenty feet of a herd of mature elephants. My hunting companion, Roy Homme, the great professional elephant hunter, agreed with me that twenty feet is as close to an African elephant as any man wants to be. Neither one of us tried this little stunt again. Neither pictures nor ivory is worth it!

One famous white hunter was saved from almost certain death when an elephant tried to kill him with his tusks. The anxious, angry animal made a tremendous thrust at the helpless hunter who had fallen to the ground. The earth was soft and the driving force of the elephant caused his tusks to stick in the ground; in his hurry to do his victim in, the tusks went on either side of the man's body; and in those few precious seconds the man scrambled away from the enraged beast while another hunter made the fatal shot.

It is true that very occasionally an elephant will leave an

unconscious enemy because he thinks his victim is dead. I talked to an African who was grabbed around the waist by a charging elephant and hurled against a tree. He was more dead than alive and hardly breathing. The elephant sniffed around the native's still body and left him for dead, after covering him with leaves and bits of brush. Indeed, a strange funeral tribute.

Arthur Neumann, who is described as one of the greatest elephant hunters who ever lived, did not escape the vengeance of the African elephant, though he managed to pull through his terrible experience. He was using a gun that was giving him trouble; and though he knew he should abandon it, it was his favorite weapon. He was hunting near Lake Rudolph, where the elephants are considered bad-tempered and aggressive. Having shot a bull, Neumann was tracking his adversary when he stumbled onto a small herd of other elephants—a couple of males and a female with her young calf. The female did not hesitate one moment; she charged immediately and Neumann, who had shot hundreds of elephants, raised his gun to fire.

Nothing happened.

He tried to reload but the cow was already on top of him; and although he tried desperately to jump out of her path, the elephant never lost track of him. He fell on his back, staring into the wicked little eyes of his enemy. In her eagerness to get at Neumann, the cow's tusks penetrated the ground on either side of the man. Here is Neumann's own account of what happened then:

> She made three distinct lunges at me, sending her left tusk through the biceps of my right arm and stabbing me between the right ribs, at the same time pounding my

chest with her head (or rather, I suppose, the thick part of her trunk between the tusks) and crushing in my ribs on the same side. At the first butt, some part of her head came in contact with my face, breaking my nose and taking patches of skin off other spots. I thought my head would be crushed, but it slipped back and was not touched again. I was wondering at the time how she would kill me; for of course I never thought anything but that the end of my hunting had come at last. What hurt most was the grinding my chest underwent. Whether she supposed she had killed me; whether it was that she disliked the smell of my blood, or whether she thought of her calf, I cannot tell; but she then left me and went her way.

Had she been wounded, nothing would have deterred her from finishing Newmann off.

A charging elephant is one of the most frightful sights and sounds in the world. Trunk curled in, emitting a blood-curdling trumpeting, the elephant comes at his opponent with an amazing burst of speed. John Taylor, the self-confessed Irish ivory poacher and renowned elephant killer, says, "There are times when the screaming, yelling, trumpeting, and smashing down of trees, as a herd stampedes, is literally paralyzing—many a hunter has described how he was totally incapable of movement until the noise died down—and other occasions when the herd is there in front of you, close by, and the next instant gone like a puff of smoke."

Of all the dangerous big-game animals, the elephant is the one most avidly sought—the ivory is valuable and men often have more greed than good sense. Because the weight of the tusks is what is important, and because in the past years the big ones have been tracked down and taken, few elephants with large, heavy tusks (a hundred pounds or more per tusk) are shot nowadays. There are still magnificent specimens reported now and then in Kenya and Tanganyika. There, tusks up to one hundred fifty pounds have been sighted, and this is a truly record trophy when one considers that the average mature elephant's ivory today runs about forty to fifty pounds; though the true sportsman will hold out for that "hundred-pounder" until the last few days of safari. Then he will lower his sights a bit and try to bag an elephant with "decent-sized ivory," usually a seventy- or eighty-pounder, if he's lucky. I have seen safari clients who have turned down an eighty-pounder because they wouldn't settle for anything less than the hundred-pound trophy. Then, toward the end of safari, they couldn't find an elephant with tusks weighing more than thirty to forty pounds. I need not say how often their thoughts returned to the eighty-pounder.

An elephant is considered mature by the time he is about twenty-five years of age—that is, when he has sizable ivory. There is some dispute about how long elephants live—some say one hundred years, some as high as one hundred fifty—but certainly, the older animals are the ones the hunter is looking for, because tusks grow slowly and it takes years and years to produce a really sizable pair. The ivory's weight and condition are also influenced by the feeding and water available in an area; thus some areas, with poor conditions, have herds with tusks that are of little interest to sportsmen.

Generally speaking, before the arrival of man the elephant had no natural enemies, except for the red safari ant—but more about this later. The elephant's tremendous bulk and strength made other animals keep a healthy distance from him. With the coming of the first settlers and the rising price of ivory on the world market, the elephant seemed doomed. The game authorities in Africa today, however, and particularly those in British East Africa, are now taking great care to build up the herds in Kenya and Tanganyika. Immediately one might say that the fault lies also with the number of sportsmen who have gone out for elephant tusks. Nothing could be further from the truth. The greatest danger to even the protected herds is the poacher, the African who hunts elephants illegally and sells the ivory to traders, who in turn smuggle the contraband out of the country. Taylor himself writes of poaching on "protected" herds—though mostly in Portuguese Africa—and recounts many incidents of running into large organized caravans and hunting parties near the Abyssinian border.

The traders (usually Indian or Arab) take the large tusks and cut them into smaller pieces which are easier to conceal, keeping only the prime sections and destroying the splintered ends and tips.

Game departments, national parks, and police wage a constant battle against the poachers and traders. The authorities do the best they can with the limited funds at their disposal, but they are badly in need of men and equipment. Every year, Arab dhows, flimsy boats, and enormous craft make their way out to the open sea with illegal elephant tusks and rhino horns. Some ivory and horn take a longer and more difficult route of travel when traders transport it thousands of miles across the continent to territories governed by individuals who have little use for smuggling regulations.

As a matter of fact, the elephant and rhino have a good many things in common. They are both vegetarians, both creatures of habit, and both victims of the tickbirds. Rhinos and elephants use their own same game trails year after year, often beaten down by their ancestors. Like the rhino, the elephant is afflicted by the tickbird. These birds hang onto the animals, picking lice off their back, and frequently burrowing into their ears in search of food.

Unlike the rhino, however, the elephant prefers to stay in large groups. There are many families in the larger herds. In their journies, elephants travel in a single file, one following the other, often a calf huddling close to its mother. They live entirely off Africa's vegetation and daily consume tremendous amounts of grass, roots, plant life, and shrubbery. Resting during the day, they travel by night, preferring, however, the early morning hours for bathing and plastering themselves with mud, which seems to be one of their greatest joys. When mud is not available, they take dust baths. It is also interesting to note that each herd has a leader to whom the other elephants defer; and it is usually his decisions which the herd obeys.

In some cases, elephants are so bound by ties of loyalty to one another that they will come to the assistance of a wounded member of the herd, particularly if it is a bull that has been shot. Usually, then, it is the cow that charges, as in the case of Neumann.

An old bull is often served by younger animals, known as pages. In the case of the older bull's being wounded, there is the likelihood that the pages will turn and charge.

The African elephant is larger and more truculent than his Asian cousin. And the Indian elephant certainly has a more pleasant disposition. It is quite normal for an African specimen to tower six or eight feet over a six-foot man and for his weight to reach six or seven tons, over ten thousand pounds. Elephants when they move are generally terribly noisy, their ears flapping, their enormous bodies rubbing up against trees, their stomachs grumbling constantly. But the crackle of a twig, a man's muffled cough, the click of a rifle or camera, the noise of the leather of a man's boots—all these alert the elephant, whose sensitive hearing makes up for his lamentable eyesight. Once on guard, he stands absolutely, rigidly still, and a moment later disappears without a sound. It is said that the secret of his silence can be attributed to the fact that the enormity of the elephant's bulk is equally distributed on his spongy feet so that he can move as elusively as a shadow.

Then there are times the elephant does not retreat, and you wish you had. The African elephant has a great sense of smell and whenever the wind warns him of a strange or dangerous scent, he raises his trunk and sniffs in all directions. An elephant's trunk in the air looks very much the same as a submarine's periscope searching for an enemy ship. The elephant uses his sense of hearing and smell to locate where he thinks an enemy is. That is why elephants make such a rush when charging. They may not have yet seen their adversary, but hope they can run down the intruder. Therefore, an important rule to remember when elephant hunting at close range is to try not to make any sudden movements regardless of how much you may want to retreat. Chances are the elephant has not seen you clearly and any movement giving your position away might be the cause of your being trampled.

I have heard people say, "As long as there are tall trees to climb, I'll be safe even from elephants." Well, before you agree with this school of thought, let me pass on a little information. Frightened people have climbed trees when trying to escape a charging elephant, and I regret to say it didn't do them the least bit of good. Either the elephant was strong enough to shake his enemy from the branches or the elephant bowled the tree over by pushing against the trunk with his forehead. Instances have been recorded where a man thought he was completely safe in a tree once he saw the elephant was able neither to shake him loose from the branches nor push the tree over. Then the man realized, to his horror, that the elephant was trumpeting for assistance from other members of the herd. The one elephant, knowing he could not do the job alone, was able actually to uproot both man and tree with the help of three other elephants. This shows how clever and revengeful this animal can be.

I believe the African fears the elephant more than any other animal because of the contempt in which the elephant holds the native. Night after night, *tembo* will come down to native *shambas* (village fields) and feast on bananas, sweet potatoes, and sugar cane. The natives are powerless to stop these raids, though a few of the braver warriors may rush out and try to drive the huge beasts off with their spears, and bows and arrows—generally most inadequate against the elephant. The majority of natives prefer to lie quietly in their huts, hoping not to attract attention, because angry or mischievous elephants have been known to level a village to the ground in a matter of minutes.

Few natives own any type of firearms; in those territories where Africans are allowed to possess rifles of any sort, the weapons are the old-fashioned muzzle-loaders or shotguns, almost useless against any big game. Their shots rarely kill elephants, only wounding them slightly, but enough to enrage them, and sometimes turn them into rogues. The elephants, in retaliation, increase their raids on villages, trample huts and crops, and often take their vengeance out on man directly.

The area around the Tana River in Northern Kenya is one of the last strongholds left for the African elephant. It is impossible to go out for a day's hunt without coming across elephants. This is one area where the Africans have about given up farming. The elephants have overrun the native *shambas* and destroyed the crops so many times that it eventually became evident to the African that he was fighting a losing battle. Elephants remain a menace, and the villagers are constantly on their guard for a raid. In this part of the country every *shamba* has a high lookout post, either in trees or on a platform built on the top of long stilts. When a herd gets too close to the village, the man on watch warns the others and the villagers seek safety. Tribesmen have discovered that sound sometimes frightens the big animals away and they use homemade noisemakers to set up a ruckus that would be the envy of Times Square on New Year's Eve.

Considering the ferocity of an elephant's charge, it has always seemed remarkable to me that in the moment of his attacks, the one thing that the elephant tries to protect is his trunk. The elephant realizes that his trunk is the "middleman" between food and himself. How could he eat without this precious utensil? So, a charging elephant will tuck his trunk between his tusks, which serve as protectors.

The best time of year to hunt elephant is from late spring through early fall. This is the dry season of the year and elephants are easier to spot because the natives purposely burn off the dry grass in order to make way for the fresh grass to grow when the rains come. Consequently, there is a good deal less risk of being trampled by a herd of elephants that have been concealed in tall grass, and the short grass, quite naturally, makes the job of tracking much easier. Further, the hunter can predetermine the elephant's whereabouts during the dry season by concentrating his efforts around the area's few water holes and running rivers.

As huge as elephants are, they can be attacked by an animal thousands of times as small as they are. The rainy season brings out millions of the dreaded species of safari ant. These ants have pincerlike jaws and stinging bites, and they have been known to attack an elephant and literally strip the hide off him. It is strange to think that so small a creature is the greatest threat to the mighty elephant, man excluded of course.

Many people are under the impression that the elephants leave the forests during the rainy season to escape the safari ants. Another theory is that the annoying sound of rain falling on leaves is a constant irritant to the elephant, and that with his hypersensitive hearing, he cannot stand the constant sound vibrations of the raindrops.

There is one theory I should like to mention in passing, that of "the elephants' graveyard." Elephants do not go to a special cemetery to die. The old elephant is generally ostracized by the herd because of not being able to keep up with the others. Elephants are constantly on the move to satisfy their food and water needs, particularly so in the dry season when water is scarce and fresh green foliage is hard to find. In some cases, an old cow elephant leaves the herd because she can no longer put up with the noise and nuisance of the young calves. A grumpy old bull does likewise, but he is also tired of being constantly challenged by the younger bulls. So he takes himself off to solitary splendor.

In a matter of time, the elephant simply dies from lack of food and water, or perhaps from poor physical condition due to an old wound or ailment. Generally speaking, though, thirst is the principal cause for the elephant's death. Heavy-flowing rivers and streams are mere trickles of water during the height of the dry season. Some dry up completely and the river beds resemble a desert. Many marshes turn into fields of dried, cracked clay. Favorite water holes show only pools of dust. Instinctively, the elephant knows that water should be in these places and yet common sense tells him differently. So the considerably weakened animal remains near these dried-up areas and patiently waits for the rains. *Tembo* dies. And in a matter of days, the vulture, hyena, stork, jackal, and wild dog packs pick the frame clean. These scavengers are often assisted by the larger carnivorous animals. The elephant's bones bleach and decay; there is nothing left save the tusks—provided rodents have not already attacked the tusks' sweet core.

And finally, nature has her say in the matter. When the rains finally do come in Africa, waters spill from the heavens for weeks at a time. It does not take long for the thirsty ground to soak up all the water it needs. Then Africa's soil can drink no more. The water spills across the earth in all directions as it floods the streams and rivers with a driving force. Bones and whatever is left of ivory tusks are picked up like twigs and churned under the angry waters. The elephant's remains are pushed deep into the muddy river bottoms and other of earth's cavities, and remain undetected by man. Few men are apt to see an elephant die a natural death, because this noble creature has the pride and dignity to want to be left alone when he feels his days are numbered. He makes every effort to make his presence unknown to man, choosing a well-concealed and quiet place to spend his last hours. Therefore, the elephant's graveyard is a place of his choosing and not that of a storyteller's.

But to get back to the question of the hunt. Hunters follow elephants by the clues given by their dung, and tracks. If fresh dung is still warm and steaming, it means that *tembo* is close by.

Nothing is ever sure in elephant hunting. The size of the elephant's tracks leads you to believe that you are following a big bull who is traveling alone and who, in all probability, will give you the prize tusks you are after. You know that the older an elephant is, the wiser he is—the more experienced and cautious—but you are willing to take the chance. So you hunt and track for days, only to come upon a single-tusker!

Or it is just as likely the large tracks may turn out to be an elephant of medium-sized ivory. Sometimes the stories you have heard and listened to in villages concern a herd of smaller tusked elephants than the giants reported by the excited Africans.

There have been more disappointments hunting elephant than any other animal I can think of.

When tracking any of the big-game animals, it is most important for camp members to be up and away by daylight. Elephants are still moving about in early morning, but by 10:00 A.M. the big herds and the great solitary bulls will be resting quietly underneath the shade trees, or whatever cover available, and they will remain that way until late afternoon. Then, in the cool of late day, the elephant will begin to travel around the countryside once more for food and water.

Let me describe an elephant hunt I was on recently, so that you can better understand the problems we experienced. Our safari party was in Northern Kenya and I was fortunate enough to have as my hunting partner Roy Homme, from Ker and Downey Safaris Limited—a senior hunter.

This particular day, we were driving along a dirt road when we spotted several elephant tracks. We parked our Land Rover under a tree and let our trackers take a closer look. Two elephants had crossed the road at daylight, and their tracks told us they were enormous bulls. We wasted no time, and off we went into semibush country. After several hours of tracking, we found warm elephant dung droppings. *Tembo* was no more than half an hour away, we reckoned.

When you are this close to elephant, every member of the tracking party must avoid making any sound that will give away the position. A crackling of a branch can send your elephant crashing into the brush. The trackers are tense. Previously, all eyes had been studying the signs on the ground; now our hunting team looked about cautiously in all directions. The last dung droppings had told us about how long ago the elephants had passed through. Now there was the possibility the elephants had stopped to browse or to rub their hides against trees.

We were moving along step by step when we heard a crackling sound directly in front of us. Our whole party froze; we knew the elephants were feeding no more than a hundred yards away. As we approached for a closer look, many more crackling sounds to our right echoed throughout the forest. Instantly every man in the party knew what was happening. The two bull elephants up ahead were joining the herd to our right.

Roy and I checked the wind and found we were still in a good position. Now we had a decision to make. We could work our way forward to get a closer look at the two elephants ahead, putting us in a more dangerous position if any of the herd caught our scent and decided to charge; or we could stay where we were and perhaps miss a chance to bring back a prize piece of ivory.

Our problem was further complicated by the fact that we had no idea how many elephants there were in the herd and in which direction they were traveling.

We never had the chance to make a final decision. The big

bodies of the two bulls crashed through some dry brush cover and ambled slowly in our direction. Both elephants were giants and had excellent ivory. They had not seen us, for there were not the usual signs of alarm: the ears out-stretched and the trunk upraised, sniffing the air. The two elephants stopped a moment and by a silent signal I could neither see nor hear, they called the other elephants in the nearby herd to join them. Now we were practically in the midst of a herd. All we could do was crouch down and remain perfectly still. I believe we also said a few silent prayers!

It is a magnificent sight to see nine bull elephants passing twenty yards away completely unaware of the presence of man. I knew from the pleased look on Roy's face that he was impressed, as I was.

When first hunting elephant, I found the hardest thing to get used to was the idea that elephants have such extremely poor eyesight. I had been told this fact by the best profes-sional elephant hunters in Africa, but somehow it was most difficult to believe whenever I came close to one of these huge beasts. It seemed impossible that such an enormous ani-mal could not see twenty yards in front of him. Provided you keep a cool head and do not move, you are comparatively safe, even at so close a range as fifty feet. However, you must be with a completely experienced hunter, and move at *his* instruction.

But now here was an elephant herd milling about us and the smallest ivory was at least sixty pounds. Roy pointed to one bull with short, thick tusks. I liked a second, which had longer but thinner ones, and my gunbearer had selected still another as the one he thought had the heaviest ivory. Again, we did not have time to make a decision, for the elephant Roy preferred wheeled around, swinging his trunk in the air.

At his sign of alarm, the other elephants milled around nervously and at that moment we fully expected a mass charge. I was convinced Roy's elephant had still not seen us, but with a sixth sense he realized danger was close by. I stress again to any who plan to hunt elephant: Do not move in a situation like this. The herd had not seen us, and any movement on our part would have meant disaster to the party.

We hardly dared breathe for five minutes, although it seemed like a lifetime. Presently the elephants quieted down and began to move off toward thicker brush, all except the one suspicious bull, who remained behind. He began to move cautiously in our direction and I knew it would be a matter of moments before we were discovered. I hoped that the elephant would turn sideways so I could have a heart shot. Brain shots are exceptionally dangerous at so close a range. The slightest miscalculation and *tembo* has claimed another victim. Even though the elephant was too close for comfort, none of us was in as dangerous a position as before the herd had ambled off. When animals hear shots, they generally run from the sound—a fortunate occurrence for hunters.

The elephant did turn, and I squeezed off the two rounds from my .470. The elephant wheeled around and went crashing through the brush directly behind him. Quickly reloading, Roy and I hurried off in his direction in time to see him crash to earth.

We were about to relax when two of our trackers pointed to our left and we saw the remaining eight bulls turn in a wide circle and head in our direction. We stooped to the ground, rifles ready, hoping against hope that eight mature elephants were not going to charge us. When the frightened lead bull spotted us, I wondered if he was thinking: Shall I lead the others in a charge, or should I seek the privacy of the forest?

He swung his body toward us, and the earth literally shook beneath us.

I swung the .470 to my shoulder, waiting for him to come a few yards closer. Roy told me he was going to take the second bull if my shots did not turn the herd. Then, with no warning, the lead bull veered sharply off to the left and the other elephants followed him, crashing through the underbrush. I have never been more relieved.

We hurried over to the elephant I had shot and found his tusks to be approximately seventy pounds apiece. My gunbearer cut off the elephant's tail with his hunting knife and gave the tail to me, an old hunting custom, showing the rightful owner of the trophy.

About those tails—I must admit that it is possible to come upon a tailless elephant. A good many rights to ownership have been cut when the animal was not actually dead, but only stunned by a poorly placed brain shot. Elephants can remain in this unconscious state for a long time. You can imagine how shocked the sportsman is when he returns with the safari crew to chop out the elephant's tusks and finds his elephant has vanished. I think it is always a good idea to put that extra shot or two in any dangerous animal you think you have killed.

When aiming at an elephant, carry one thing in mind. The hide is a formidable protective covering. In firing, it is essential you hit a vital organ. But here again you are in trouble. The brain is small and the skull protecting it thick and solid. The head shot is NOT recommended. The elephant's frontal slope makes it most difficult to penetrate the brain from a facing position. A well-placed shoulder shot will penetrate the heart. If your aim is slightly off, and you shoot the elephant in the lungs, you will still have your trophy.

Most people who have been on safari will run into an African tribesman who has his favorite myth concerning the African elephant. The same story regarding a legendary giant elephant keeps cropping up. Veterans of the bush with many years hunting experience have spent weeks trying to hunt that BIG ONE with a-hundred-and-eighty-pound tusks. More times than not, those tusks have been in the mind of a native, rather than on the front of an elephant.

One time I devoted three weeks hunting one giant elephant. He, too, was a legend. Local villagers swore that they had personally seen this monster of all monsters. They described his tracks and how his ivory tusks had almost turned black with age. I was told this particular elephant had such enormous tusks that he had to prop them up against lower limbs of trees because their weight was too heavy for him to hold them up for any length of time. I was further told the elephant traveled alone for great distances and that he could enter a small clumb of trees and vanish into thin air.

The tribesmen warned me that no white man would ever be able to shoot this elephant, for here was an animal smarter than the white man. Here was an animal who could tell when a hunter was within five miles of him. "Wasn't it true," said the village elders, "that whenever other hunters had tried to track down this elephant, he would disappear off the face of the earth and the day the hunters left the area, the elephant would reappear? Surely God must be on his side."

Tom Lithgow, a fine professional hunter, agreed to hunt with me and see if we could not seek out this mystery elephant. Because we had only three weeks, we tried using several villages as centers for scouting parties. Tom and I decided that we would be wasting time if we hunted with any one particular scouting team, for then other scouting groups would not be able to reach us in time, should they spot the legendary elephant first. So we devised a plan. Each group of scouts was told to report back to our central camp the moment any trace of our elephant came to sight. Well, of course there were all kinds of reports about giant trophies of other game, but nothing at all on our elephant. Day after day passed and we were terribly discouraged. Then word came in.

A scout from one team came running into camp, exhausted. Between gasps he told us that his team had seen "the mightiest of all elephants" earlier the same morning. The elephant was feeding in the next valley eight miles away. His companions remained behind, watching the elephant's movements. Our scout told us that we could drive part of the way in our Land Rover. Tom and I wasted no further time. A quick check of water and food rations, flashlights, snake kit, ammunition, and rifles and off we went.

When we arrived with our guide, the rest of his tracking team had vanished. The scout could not understand where his team companions had gone, unless, of course, this mighty elephant's sixth sense had warned him of man's presence and he had fled for cover. Tom and I agreed the best thing to do was to start off immediately in the general direction our trackers had last seen the elephant. We were on a mountain slope, and we scanned the area closely with our binoculars.

As I studied one area of dense undergrowth, a likely cover for elephant, I spotted the rest of our scouting team. They were working their way toward the same dense cover and had stopped at a tall tree. One of the boys was climbing it for a better look around, or so I first thought. Actually, he was signaling to us with a hand mirror.

We answered his sun flashes, took one last bearing and practically tumbled down into the valley.

Two hours later we reached our tracking team. The elephant was last seen in the thick cover directly ahead, but since then a herd of elephants had entered the same area. No one was more disappointed than myself. This legendary elephant had a reputation of not staying around other elephants, and this herd must surely have frightened him off.

Nevertheless, we told our scouts we would work our way into the thicket and hope to pick up the elephant's trail. Our plan wasn't exactly greeted joyously by the Africans. We knew the danger of going into a thickly forested area amongst a herd of elephants, especially when there were cows and calves to consider. However, sometimes we all do foolish things because of disappointment or impatience.

Off we went slowly into the thicket. We were able to skirt silently by the elephant herd as they browsed no more than two hundred feet from us. When we finally reached semiopen ground, the sun was beginning to slip behind the mountains. Now I truly felt discouraged, because not only had the elephant beaten us, but nature had as well.

Then one of the scouts pointed excitedly to another patch of thick brush about four hundred feet away. I caught a glimpse of the disappearing rump of the largest elephant I had ever seen. This was a race against animal and light. We dared not proceed as cautiously as we would have normally, because in twenty minutes it would be dark. We crossed the semi-clearing in a half crouch. As Tom and I reached the outskirts of the thicket, we paused to listen for any sounds the elephant might be making. We heard a cracking sound up ahead and to our right. As we entered the dense underbrush again, the light was so poor that I could hardly make out the outlines of the men with me.

Then I saw my elephant and knew that he was no phantom, no ghost, no legend, but certainly one of the few magnificent elephants left in the world today. His tusks were thick and black, curled up in a mighty swoop at the tips. The elephant showed no sign of alarm, and must have thought he had fooled man once again.

Because the light was so poor, I wanted to move a bit closer to be sure of a fatal shot. I could only see the dim outline of this magnificent animal. My whole body had become wet with perspiration and the water rolled off my forehead, stinging my eyes. My trackers were silent, but were furiously motioning me to shoot. They did not realize that I could no longer see the elephant.

He was standing in one spot which bathed him in darkness and for those few moments I had the strangest feeling he was being protected by something greater and more powerful than I could understand. Then another stroke of fortune occurred for the elephant. The nearby herd had decided to push on and were headed in our direction. Perhaps it was a cow's shrill cry looking for her youngster, or a command from one of the bulls for the herd to keep together, but the whole herd began to infiltrate the area. The trumpeting went on for at least three minutes. Even above this noise, we heard a crashing of trees close by which meant our trophy had disappeared into the African night. So Tom and I had joined a long list of hunters who had failed to shoot this trophy; but, as far as I know, we were the only two white men to see the "mightiest of all elephants."

CHAPTER VI

FARO—
The Rhinoceros

I have a hunch that the day a rhino is born and opens his eyes, he hates the world. The rhino is the bully of the jungle. He is instinctively mean and short-tempered. Rhinos will fight among themselves and with any other animal, except the elephant. Most rhinos wear open wounds or scars from combat.

Of course, I am speaking of the black rhino. There is a white rhino, actually gray in color, which is completely different than his cousin, the black rhino. The white rhino is a peaceful, grass-eating animal, larger in body than the black species, and has an upper lip that is pointed. The white rhino is easygoing by nature and perhaps this is the main reason he has become practically extinct. They are now protected by game laws throughout Africa today. Natives used to hunt the white rhino because they could approach this animal without fearing a charge. But they would soon be up a tree if they tried the same tactics on the black one.

Since the black rhino is shootable by game laws, let's find out more about this destructive "armored tank."

Besides being antisocial, *faro* is a conformist in the extreme, a combination I have often found rather amusing. He will follow the same well-beaten path for years; and at times he has been known to go right through the center of a safari camp (at night) when the camp was pitched across his favorite game trail.

Rhino goes to his watering hole in the evening and early morning, returning to the same spots day after day, year after year; he is so tied to his love of habit that he even goes to the same places to dung. When the sun rises, he makes for a shady spot and lies down. Often he'll dig a shallow trench. Like most African game animals he sleeps during the day—although doze would be the better description, for he is constantly on the alert, one eye open and watching. He has his own vigilance committee as well: a small phalanx of green tickbirds which buzz about him in search of lice and warn him if any enemy is in sight. Tickbirds make life miserable for the rhino, for they are in a constant search for the parasites on which they feed, burrowing in and out of his ears, nose, and attacking his skin ceaselessly. One reason rhinos are so fond of their mud baths is that the ticks leave them alone while they are wallowing, and the mud soothes some of the little smarting wounds the birds have inflicted.

The rhino is an ugly beast, short, squat, with small ears and a snub nose. He is shortsighted and cannot identify most enemies until he sees a movement. The average size of a rhino is about twelve feet in height, the average weight around four thousand pounds. The mouth of the rhino is so tough that he has no trouble masticating thorns. He scrapes bark from a tree by means of his horns. He has a habit of chewing like a horse, spitting out the fiber when finished with the sweeter part of the bark. Oftentimes, while tracking, I have come across bits of bark fiber still wet with saliva.

Rhino is Africa's best water diviner. The instant he smells water, he sets to work, digging frantically until there is a small hole from which he can get the moisture he needs. Even elephants, who are reputed to have a sixth sense about locating water, will take a back seat to the rhino, patiently waiting until *faro* has dug a hole, drunk and departed, before moving in to satisfy themselves.

The rhino hates to be disturbed. He will also charge seemingly without the slightest provocation, or merely because his temper has been ruffled. The charge, once begun, however, is completed in almost total blindness. The rhino charges in a straight line and cannot see his target because when the head is down, the eyes have a view only of the area that is being traversed. Even when the rhino pauses to search out the enemy, he is handicapped by extremely poor vision.

Nevertheless, *faro* is an extremely dangerous animal. Stonehamd, the famous English big-game hunter, believes the rhino has killed more men (not hunters, but men) than any other animal in Africa. Unsuspecting natives are constantly charged by rhinos, and rhinos will make these charges from a bush which has completely covered them from view.

In the Narok Hospital in Northern Masailand, the medical staff told me more natives ended up there because of mauling by rhinos than by any other animal. I have seen that this is true, particularly in areas where natives graze a lot of livestock.

Their cattle, goats, and sheep like to browse around in dense brush areas. Not only do they feed there, but these animals enjoy the shade the cover offers. Therefore, when the native goes in search of his livestock, he is apt to come across a rhino resting in the same thick underbrush where his livestock has been grazing. Unfortunately for the native, the dense country offers few chances for escape.

Another reason for the high fatality list attributed to rhino is that people are apt to underestimate this vicious brute. Admittedly, *faro* has poor eyesight. But this is his only shortcoming. I have often heard the story that rhinos are clumsy, awkward, and slow in their movements, and therefore easy to run from. I do not suggest you try to do this. Africans and Europeans are resting in graves today who could run a lot faster than you and I. They thought they could outsmart rhino, not realizing this beast, standing five feet at the shoulder, can turn on a dime.

As a matter of fact, a sure way of inviting disaster with any wild charging animal is to turn your back on him. He is faster, and certainly physically stronger, than you are. If you have to run, keep a clear head when you do so. Do not necessarily choose the closest tree, but one whose limbs you can reach. Never run for rock protection unless you can scramble under a ledge or into a crevice where the animal cannot follow. If an animal is charging you and there is not a chance to escape, dodge to your left or right, but only at the last moment, giving the animal less chance to change direction.

Rhinos are fairly easy to track. The rhino's middle toe is larger than the other two and this simplifies identification. François Somer claims that the rhino is more susceptible to bullet wounds than the other Big Five because the bullet flattens out against the thick hide and causes the animal to bleed profusely—but I wouldn't *count* on that if I were you. The rhino has a lot more blood than you have time during a charge.

One way to hunt rhino is to camp in an area where there is thick underbrush, preferably thorn trees. Rhinos love to feed on these and this kind of country also offers them excellent cover. The safari client gets up very early in the morning. By sunrise, he is away from camp and examining game trails, sandy paths, dirt roads, and dry river bottoms, actually any place where fresh rhino tracks can be easily detected. Usually by now, *faro* has already satisfied his thirst and is making his way back to thicker cover so that he can rest unmolested. Chances are he will not be traveling fast, but at a steady pace, nibbling at thorn trees and tree bark as he ambles along. Nevertheless, the average pace of a rhino is a good deal faster than the average man's, and once the tracks have been found, the sportsman should waste no time. Unlike the elephant who will pause for long periods at a time while feeding, the rhino stays on the move.

While he works himself into thicker cover, *faro* leaves droppings of dung. The freshness of the spoor will give an idea of how close he is. As the hunting party approaches closer, there are other signs: pieces of wood freshly snapped as his enormous body pushed itself through an obstruction, chewed bark left on the ground, and always the smell. The rhino has a musky odor which is unlike any other animal's. In many instances your nose will give you warning before your eyes and ears.

The native trackers and gunbearers search the sky and surrounding trees and bushes in the hope of spotting the tiny tickbird. There is nothing tenser than the moments after the birds have been spotted. No words are spoken. Anything to be said is done in sign language, from tracker to hunter to gunbearer. Nerves are on edge, eyes strain into the dense underbrush. Then someone signals a slight movement ahead. There, in the thick cover, a rhino is waiting.

No matter how many times you hunt rhino, you never expect the speed with which he rises and charges. The head is lowered, the horns aimed at your body, and this is the time to shoot and shoot well. At this range you cannot afford to miss.

Because the head is lowered, the best place to aim is the back of the neck. This shot is deadly. The shoulder shot is also an excellent one, provided the rhino is not charging straight at you, or has not yet lowered his head during a frontal charge.

There are several reasons for this. If you shatter a shoulder, you cripple the animal and make any further lightning charges impossible. Also, a good shot will hit the big arteries at the head of the heart and fatally wound the animal.

Many hunters will suggest the frontal chest shot when there's some distance between you and the rhino. Aim high instead of low. If you shoot too low, the part of the heart you want to hit—the top part—is usually missed. There are endless reports of animals shot through the heart who continue their charge, a terrifying sight to the waiting sportsman who is sure he made a killing shot. But most of these shots have been through the lower heart where, while the animal was mortally wounded, he still had strength to continue his assault.

Some rhinos will run away when they feel their privacy has been disturbed. Then you spend another two hours tracking *faro*, but first allowing him a good head start. Then he thinks you are no longer on his trail. But don't become discouraged. It is rare when you disturb a rhino more than two or three times that the animal continues to move on. His bad disposition rules against so peaceful an action. After several of these rude interruptions, he will come at you madder than ever. Then watch out.

The sportsman wants the triumph of his trophy; the African and Asian are interested in the magic power of the horn, believed to have special attributes which recommend it as an aphrodisiac. The horn is ground into a precious dust and mixed into a potion. African poachers sell these horns to traders and make more money with one horn than they would working several months on a European farm, so it is no wonder there is a brisk illicit smuggling business going on.

I use the term "rhino horn," but this is not entirely accurate. The horn is actually a solidly pressed hair tissue that comes to a sharp point. Rarely will you find a rhino horn larger than twenty-six inches today, and anything more than that is considered a prize trophy indeed. The average rhino horn taken on safari is from eighteen to twenty-two inches.

It is not unusual for a rhino to charge a hunting car; and if he hits the moving vehicle at the proper angle, his tremendous strength and force can overturn the car. Once the rhino is angry, he does not care whom or what he is attacking. Some amazed railroad engineers have reported that these ill-tempered brutes have charged headlong into their trains. This might be a good thing to remember when you are in rhino country. Certainly you do not look as menacing as a steaming locomotive.

Those sportsmen who are fortunate enough to find rhino in open country have an easier time bagging their trophy. As I previously mentioned, the rhino has exceedingly poor eyesight, so he can be approached at fairly close range. *Faro* will probably "feel" man's presence, a kind of sixth sense wild game animals have, before he sees the hunter. More than likely, the hunter is only a blur and not clearly outlined to the rhino. He will snort, kick up some dust and make a "bluff" charge. *Faro* is a natural bully by instinct and from past experience he knows most "blurs" run from him when he puts on this act. Yet when properly challenged in the open, he won't turn down a fight. If the hunter stands his ground, the rhino may or may not offer several additional "bluff" charges. Finally the exasperated beast will emit his angry snort and on he comes. Experienced hunters can readily tell that this time the rhino is deadly serious in his attack. Now's the perfect time for a chest shot while *faro* approaches with his head still up. Use the .470 and he'll never know what hit him.

I remember a recent experience I had with the rhino in the Narok area of Kenya. Actually our safari was there to hunt lions. We did agree that if time permitted we would investigate a thickly wooded area sitting off by itself in the middle of some flat, rolling plains. I guess the best way to describe the area is that it seemed like a wooded oasis in the middle of a green desert. The natives name this place *Hoteli ya Kafaro*, which means Hotel of the Rhino. Few African tribesmen dared invade this miniature forest, the exception being a group of Masai warriors who were forced to take their cattle on the wooded outskirts so that their livestock could drink from natural springs.

Early one morning we cut across the Masai plains in our Land Rover and headed toward *Hoteli ya Kafaro*. We arrived at this wooded oasis and were fortunate to find three Masai warriors herding their cattle. We began to fire questions at them.

Yes, they knew there were many rhinos in the thick cover. They had heard them that morning crashing their way through the thornbushes. I asked the Masai if they had actually seen any of the rhinos. They looked at me, surprised and frightened, assuring me they would not go in there, that they had no wish to get close enough to *faro* to see him.

It was impossible for us to take our Land Rover any farther so we began walking on the outskirts of the thorn thickets until we saw signs of fairly fresh spoor. The tracks told us it was a huge male rhino and that's all we needed to know. My favorite tracker, Masyoka, and his two assistants Shabani and Wariyo practically put their noses to the ground and led off the procession.

In the excitement of the stalk we did not realize how thickly wooded the area was. I had also ignored a most important rule when hunting. Never put yourself in a position where your immediate natural surroundings—such as sharp thorn branches, thick overhead foliage, and masses of vines—command most of your attention. These annoying barriers keep your hands busy as you try to track, and thick cover offers the additional danger of camouflaging your trophy so well that you may not be able to get off a shot should the animal ambush and charge you.

By now we found ourselves having to do exactly this, using our hands to separate thornbushes from our face and body when the same hands should be ready to hold a rifle for an immediate shot. A crashing sound exploded behind us, which must have been a rhino we had passed without knowing he was so close.

This rhino, rushing through the area with tremendous racket, seemed to be the signal for all the rhinos to do the same. All around us we heard the same crashing noises and I am sure it was not our imagination that heard snorts uncomfortably close to where we were crouched. The thorn trees and other foliage surrounding us were so thick that I was afraid these same branches would deflect any cartridge that was fired. I knew perfectly well that when hunting in such unfavorable conditions there is only time for one correct shot; that is, if you want to walk away and tell the story.

I have been surrounded by elephants when silently working my way through a herd in order to come up close to the animal with the largest ivory; I have silently knelt like a statue in an open area where buffaloes were grazing all around me; and you may remember from the lion chapter that I was once completely encircled by a pride of lions. But this was the first and I hope the last time that I ever will be surrounded by at least a dozen snorting locomotives angrily running in all directions.

A cow and her calf plunged past one of the trackers, knocking him down, although I doubt if the rhino even saw him. Another cow snorted her rage at my gunbearer, who was trying desperately to scramble out of her way. The rhino was so angry that she missed Kamuya and bashed into a tree instead. At first I thought it was her poor eyesight, but when she backed off and butted the tree again, I realized that she was just plain hopping mad.

Then it was my turn to be a circus acrobat. I was busy watching for a rhino crashing somewhere off to our left. As it turned out, I was too busy watching. I heard one of the boys shout a cry of warning, and I did not even have to turn around to know a rhino was coming straight in my direction. My feet started moving the moment I heard the boys cry out. Later they told me I looked very funny, swinging like a baboon from the tree limb.

We hardly dared breathe for minutes, but finally we inched our way back on our hands and knees. It took three hours to return to the edge of this wooded area, and only when I saw open sunlight did I feel relieved. I never finished exploring the interior of *Hoteli ya Kafaro*, nor do I intend to—unless there is some way I can get a Sherman tank up to the Narok area.

A final word about *faro*. Should you ever hunt this animal, remember his ugly disposition and complete lack of fear. Before you challenge the rhino, you should have hunted many of Africa's other animals. Become confident of your shooting ability, and be well acquainted with how animals can blend into nature's background. Then, go after *faro*—and I hope you will find that old-timer with the forty-inch horn.

CHAPTER VII

MBOGO—
The African Cape Buffalo

The African Cape buffalo is the thinker among the Big Five, the crafty sizer-up of a situation, terrain, enemy, the problems before him. He will stand absolutely still, looking at all the difficulties before him, like a general mapping out military maneuvers, and then, if provoked enough, he will attack, certain that he is in charge of the situation—but then and only then. He does not charge in a wild rush of hysterical anger. If there is some distance between *mbogo* and man, the Cape buffalo keeps his head high and his eyes on the man. He does not lower his massive horns for the attack until they are practically within striking distance. His charge is motivated by the most terrible and fearsome of all instincts: cold, calculated revenge.

An elephant may or may not detour when a bullet strikes him in the head. A Cape buffalo will not alter his charge. If you don't kill him or seriously cripple him, and there is an ounce of strength left in him, he will struggle up and charge with renewed vengeance, determined to kill you.

The African Cape buffalo does not charge a man because he enjoys doing so; like most animals, he does so only to ensure his privacy, for he asks nothing more than to be left

99

alone to enjoy his grazing and mud bathing. Buffaloes that charge without apparent provocation are undoubtedly old rogues suffering from scars of previous encounters, or animals who have been startled and feel they are cornered.

From a distance, as he grazes placidly at the edge of the plains, the Cape buffalo gives an impression of gentleness and docility. But a wounded buffalo is the most dangerous animal in the world. If you ask professional hunters their opinion of *mbogo*, a large percentage will answer that he is the worst to deal with of the Big Five—"once he is wounded."

The buffalo stands about six feet high and weighs over a ton, with a horn spread of thirty-five to sixty inches. An animal must be well over twenty years old to produce really large horns. The depletion of the herds in recent times has made the shooting of a buffalo with a horn spread over forty-five inches unlikely.

I have read stories about "hunters" who were charged by an entire herd of Cape buffalo. The buffalo were not molested or harmed in any way, other than a distant intrusion of their privacy. "Absolute rot!" is my comment about these hair-raising tales. You try to approach a herd. The Cape buffalo will run, but it will be in the opposite direction. Sometimes experienced hunters and photographers are able to approach a herd at close quarters without stampeding the buffaloes. They are able to do so by moving slowly, remaining motionless a few moments, and then advancing a few more steps.

If you are ever in a similar position, you will recognize the following behavior pattern of *mbogo*. As soon as your presence is detected, one or two of the older bulls will remain behind on guard while the herd ambles away. Henceforth, every movement of yours is watched with suspicion. Pay particular attention to the herd bulls. They are tough customers and have not remained behind to exchange pleasantries. If a herd bull thinks you have overstayed your welcome, he shakes his massive horns and expresses his anger in snorts. That is the time to remain absolutely still unless you want a Cape buffalo breathing down your neck. Naturally, if you want the herd bull as a trophy, you are in a perfect position for a shot. If you don't want to bring him down, then I suggest you discreetly retire before the buffalo decides he wants you as a trophy.

The Cape buffalo is a creature of water and marshes. Not unlike domestic cattle, the African buffalo enjoys the tasty grass in meadows, tender plants at the forest's edge, and the sweet crops natives cultivate in their fields. These animals feed at night and are rarely seen near villages until after dark. Then they visit the village fields (*shambas*) and have a feast. Early morning finds them returning to take shelter where they can find shade from the hot African sun. After two hours of daylight, the Cape buffaloes are nowhere to be seen. They might be bedded down in thick foliage around the river or perhaps the herd has decided to spend the day in the high grass at the swamp's edge. No matter, they wish to be left alone. They do not ask for company and try to remain hidden from man and beast.

Their scent, hearing, and eyesight are keen. I am sure I have bypassed many a Cape buffalo. The animal is intelligent and cunning. If he feels he is well hidden and safe, he will remain for hours in cover without moving a muscle. That is why it is so important to spot Cape buffaloes in the early hours of morning before their herd has chosen its resting place.

When the herd is at rest grazing, there is a good deal of grunting, snorting, kicking up of dust, rattling of horns. But let an enemy appear and the herd almost as one animal closes in on itself and silently disappears.

Professional hunters point out again and again that accidents are constantly happening because hunters new to the game underestimate the animal's strength and slyness. Fooled by the mild manner of *mbogo* as he grazes peacefully in swamp meadows or on the fringe of a forest, the hunter thinks to himself, Oh this buffalo business has been exaggerated. You know how these stories get built up.

He begins to blaze away, and three or four wounded and enraged animals have made for cover. To my mind the only thing worse than having to go into cover for a wounded buffalo is having to go in for two or three. Yet time and again, one hears stories of safari clients who shoot at more than one. Their professional hunter then goes into the dense undercover to track one, only to be attacked and killed by another.

Let me stress again, the buffalo is particularly dangerous because his thinking powers are human. Sometimes he will pretend to be dead and when the inexperienced hunter does not take the trouble to put an extra shot or two into his "dead" trophy before walking up to it, he is apt to find the buffalo suddenly coming to life and making one final effort to toss his enemy.

The Cape buffalo will also double back on his tracks so he can cleverly ambush his adversary. When a hunter is following up a wounded buffalo, this is one of the few game animals that can make a man with a rifle feel that it is he who is really being hunted. Buffaloes have the frightening habit of being able to remain absolutely still regardless of how hurt they are. They know how to hide their massive gray-black bodies behind cover that would appear unlikely to conceal animals half their size.

One more important point about hunting the Cape buffalo. You cannot stop a charge from him simply by firing and hitting him. The horns make a brain shot practically impossible because *mbogo's* horns form a protective armor against the penetration of the bullet. The "boss," or horn formations, cover the frontal forehead area. Try to aim for the chest if the buffalo is running toward you and he still has his head high. If he has already lowered the head, try to aim slightly over the nostrils. I cannot stress how important those first shots are; for if a buffalo is not stopped immediately, you are in serious, deadly danger. *And, use a heavy enough caliber rifle.* I like a .450 number two, or a .470, the same weapon I use on elephant.

Most men who have been fortunate to live after being charged and caught by an African Cape buffalo will agree their lives were spared mostly by luck. Many a hunter has had the unpleasant experience of not being able to bring down a charging buffalo, even though certain the initial shot was fatal. As the buffalo charged, ready to toss, he came crashing down on his terrified opponent. Actually, what has happened is that the animal is charging in his death spasm. The last spurt of energy carries him almost to the hunter.

Other people who were tossed and lived to tell about it kept a cool head and did not move after they hit the ground. This saved their lives. For the buffalo—after a few investigating snorts—leaves his victim, thinking him dead. Then there are a few very lucky people who have helplessly faced a charging buffalo and have seen the animal change his mind at the last minute and veer off. There is absolutely no explanation for this, and it runs contrary to all that we know about a Cape buffalo's behavior.

I should like to emphasize that the shoulder shot is an excellent one, either initially or in the *first* moment of the charge. Shattering the shoulder always incapacitates an animal; but with the buffalo, there's a good chance of a spinal concussion.

The best time for hunting Cape buffalo is in early morning or late afternoon. You can count on *mbogo* not being far from water. Buffaloes enjoy soaking themselves in cool, mud swamps. If a river or stream is nearby buffaloes slip in and out of the water all day. Often they rest in tall grasses and thick jungle foliage. Only when the sun sinks behind the mountain does the herd leave cover. Now is the time buffaloes think about moving from one area to another in search of new feed.

I still do not know any better way of hunting buffalo than taking time and trouble to ask local villagers where they have last seen *mbogo*. Whenever entering a new area, I prefer to sacrifice one day's hunting and catch up on local news from the local villagers. Actually the time is not really lost; it pays off in the long run.

When I visit these local villages for information, I invariably hear about "the largest buffalo we have ever seen and he raided the fields only last night." No doubt this buffalo will be a big bull with a good horn spread, but I don't raise my hopes for a world-record trophy. Africans are apt to stretch the truth if they think the *"Bwana's* bullet medicine" will get rid of an animal ruining their planted crops.

Buffalo herds rotate their visits to the village *shambas.* Although constantly on the move, they do not wander far from any given area. For instance, they may visit a village every third or fourth night, moving off to another *shamba* half a mile away. Of course if the herd becomes frightened by organized native force, or heavy gunfire from a party on safari, then they will move out of the area completely.

When you hunt buffalo, it is wise to hire local villagers by the day since they are familiar with every tree, bush, and path in their own area. These local trackers rise before daylight and check the places they think buffaloes may be feeding. Scooting up tall trees like monkeys, they wait until dawn when, from their high posts, they can usually spot the herds feeding in the area. The natives work in teams of twos and threes, sending one man back to report while the others remain at their tree posts as observers. Should the buffaloes elect to move out of the area before safari members arrive at the scene, the sentries can spot and keep track of their movements.

However, all safaris have their "bad days" and Cape-buffalo hunting provides its share of disappointments. Buffalo herds can vanish overnight, seemingly, into thin air and then you must spend the rest of the day searching the area for tracks.

The trick of buffalo hunting is to cut off the herd before it enters thick underbrush, for once in underbrush, you will find it impossible to hunt. After you have located fresh tracks, you must stalk *mbogo* downwind and very quietly. An interesting little device for telling which way the wind is blowing is used by many hunters. They fashion a little bag of ashes which, with a tap, shows which way the wind is working. But caution and silence are the two watchwords; the sound of a rifle clicking, a whisper, the slapping away of a fly, even someone breathing heavily, can give the position away.

If you are fortunate, the herd will lie down on the outskirts of thicker jungle cover. If the buffalo you have picked is about to settle down as you approach him, use patience and wait for an hour or so for your buffalo to go to sleep. You can make a closer approach and can be certain of getting a better shot.

Trackers are usually sent in a wide circle behind the dozing buffalo. They climb trees and start shouting and striking stones together. The buffalo jumps to his feet angrily. If you have planned properly, he will move in the opposite direction from which the noise is coming—that is, toward you. The hunter is now in position for the perfect kill.

Yet many times things spoil the shot. The racket of the trackers may drive other buffaloes out of the surrounding thickets.

This happened to me once. As a lone bull galloped out of a thicket, I brought him down with a shoulder shot and then one in the neck. As I left my cover, I turned to see a herd of twelve buffaloes fifty yards away and directly behind me. They had been lying in tall grass and had come over to investigate the bellowing of the dying buffalo. I placed two shots over their heads and a third shot kicked up some dust in front of the buffalo closest to me. All the twelve galloped off in the opposite direction, but I might have been in the position of facing a herd charge, a thought no hunter relishes. I tell this story to stress one point. Never forget the biggest danger in big-game hunting may very well be from animals in the area you cannot see and not from the animal you are stalking.

Now let me repeat one thing since we are talking about rules of safety. Try to avoid tracking this animal into dense underbrush. If he is wounded, of course your professional hunter has no choice.

Consequently, the most important shot in big-game hunting is the first one. Take your time, steady your rifle sights on a vital part of the animal's body, and squeeze the trigger.

Have another rifle ready at all times and make sure you are in a position for a clean shot. Follow these rules and you have an excellent chance of telling your hunting experiences to your grandchildren.

There are two very famous stories about the African Cape buffalo often repeated around the campfire. A few years ago, runs the first, a hunter spotted a fine specimen of horn over forty-five inches. In the excitement, he made a bad error: he went into thick underbrush where a clear, clean shot was next to impossible. Although the gunbearer pleaded, the hunter would not listen. He had made up his mind he was going to have that trophy. The buffalo, meantime, worked himself deeper and deeper into the brush, trying to get away from his pursuer.

The light was very poor; a good shot was impossible, but the man was determined. He fired at a dim outline. As the enraged buffalo turned to return the challenge, the hunter fired twice more. The buffalo paid no attention.

At this point the gunbearer and the two trackers took to their heels and fled for their lives. The hunter panicked and ran for cover under a nearby rock barrier. This rock formation, the story goes, had a jutting ledge and the hunter thought he could roll under the ledge and protect himself from the charge of the buffalo. To his relief, he found he could get nearly all his body under the ledge save one small portion of his foot, which did not worry him because it was heavily booted.

The buffalo was furious, snorting and stamping, hooking his horns against the ledge, trying to get at the hunter. Finally the animal saw that it was impossible.

What happened next, we can only surmise from the evidence that was gathered later. The man must have had a most horrifying shock when he felt the buffalo start tearing at his boot leather with its grinding teeth. The next thing the man must have felt was a hard, raspy tongue on the sole of his foot. The buffalo was licking the skin away from the only part of the hunter's body he could get at.

The trackers who fled returned with a game warden and they found the hunter under the ledge, the buffalo quite dead next to him. Both had bled to death.

I know no other story which could more strongly demonstrate the African Cape buffalo's cunning and determination for revenge.

The second story that comes to mind happened to two settler friends of mine during a hunt right after World War II.

They were tracking three fine bulls in Southern Tanganyika. They wanted to get a closer look at the buffaloes before deciding which one they would take for a trophy. As they quietly approached the three bulls, now settled under some shade trees, some baboons overhead screeched and gave away the hunters' position. Two of the bulls galloped off to the left while the largest stood his ground and challenged the intruders. One man fired two shots at the buffalo's chest. I am sure he did not take the proper time to aim, for neither shot brought the buffalo down. One snort and the animal charged.

Both my friends were able to climb a tree before feeling the points of the buffalo's horns. Unfortunately, in their scramble, they dropped their rifles. They were up the tree, unarmed, but safe. But the buffalo was at the bottom, wounded and determined.

My friends stayed in that tree two nights and two days. Each day, the buffalo became weaker and yet would not give an inch. He just raised his eyes and stared balefully at his enemies.

Both men were lucky to have canteens attached to their belts and they were able to wet their mouths occasionally. There was water near for the buffalo also, perhaps some five hundred yards away, but the animal would not go near it. Occasionally he would look at the stream, and it seemed to my friends that the buffalo was trying to make the decision whether to leave the position he had taken up to get the water he desperately needed or remain fixed where he was.

Once or twice the buffalo started toward the stream, but each time, when he heard both men start to climb down for their rifles, he whirled around and rushed the tree again.

On the third night, this courageous animal died. I think this is a great tribute to the African Cape buffalo's perseverance. He denied himself the water he needed in order to live. At any time he could have escaped in the nearby bush.

I shall never forget one experience I had with buffalo, which nearly had a most unhappy ending—not for the buffalo, but for me.

Our safari was camped near the Kina River in Northern Kenya, excellent country for buffalo. One evening while we were having supper, the head camp boy, Matiso, announced that some Africans from a nearby village had come to pay their respects, and to ask a favor. I told Matiso to offer them some antelope steaks and to tell them we would be out to talk to them presently.

In almost a matter of moments, Matiso was back to tell us that the natives had politely refused the offer. All they wanted was to talk. Whenever an African refuses freshly killed meat, he must have something terribly important on his mind. We asked the village elders into our mess tent; and from their worried, preoccupied expressions, we could sense they were in serious trouble.

They all started talking at once. It seemed there were two rogue buffaloes in the area and these animals had raided their villages every night for the past three weeks. The buffaloes did not belong to the regular herds usually found near the villages, and the Africans described them as devils. Two of the buffaloes had already attacked three of their villagers, and had severely damaged crops as well. What they wanted to know was whether we would return to their village immediately and shoot the buffaloes.

It is difficult to explain game laws to an African. I am sure they did not understand that we would not be able to go after the buffaloes until morning. We told them that only game wardens or specially appointed government officials have permission to hunt animals at night. We promised, however, that we would be at their village the following morning before first light, and would spend our time hunting these rogues.

The village elders thanked us, but I could see their puzzlement and the disappointment in their eyes. I know what they were thinking: Why couldn't these white men come and kill the buffalo now? They had seen white *Bwanas* hunt in fields before at night, shining bright lights in the buffaloes' eyes and shooting the blinded animals easily. Did not this make more sense than risking one's life during the day?

As we promised, daylight found us at the village. At the time, Tom Lithgow was my safari hunting partner. We had quietly worked ourselves down to the *shambas* while it was still dark. We could see the dim outlines of both buffaloes moving across the fields. They seemed to be slowly heading back toward the river half a mile away. Since they did not appear to be alarmed, we decided to give the buffaloes a good head start and track them from a distance.

By now it was daylight so we kept close to the ground as

we followed them. To our surprise, the buffaloes turned away from the river and entered some nearby thick cover. We had not counted on this, and now were in a most difficult position to continue without being detected. We had no choice but to wait behind some tall grass tufts and let the buffaloes work themselves farther into the underbrush.

Ten minutes later, we went into the dense foliage after the *mbogo*. They could not have picked a better spot for them, nor a worse one for us. The vegetation was so thick that we could hardly see four feet in front of us; and almost every step we took made some slight sound. We heard the buffaloes up ahead. We could tell from the dry cracking sound of branches that these animals had not yet settled down to rest.

Tom and I were on our hands and knees crawling through a particularly thick undergrowth of branches and vines. We had not heard the buffaloes for a few moments, and we assumed this might be a good time to close up the distance between us.

We had come to a spot where we were able to stand up, when we heard some extremely loud snapping sounds and the wall of foliage directly in front of us began to shake. The first thought I had was that the buffaloes had seen us and were coming out for a charge. Tom and I both had our rifles ready to fire when we got the surprise of our lives. Something came charging out of the bush in front of us, only it was not our two buffalo. A tremendous bull elephant, and a very angry one at that, was running us down.

Tom and I fired both barrels practically at the same time. We needed all the fire power possible at so close a range; for the elephant would surely have killed one or both of us had we not been able to stop him instantly with a frontal brain shot. I remember there was hardly time to fire a second shot when the elephant crashed to the ground on his front knees. The whole earth shook as his body flopped over on its side. In the excitement, I am sure there were other sounds—particularly those of the two buffaloes escaping. However, I must confess the buffaloes were the farthest things from my mind at the time.

This bull had fairly decent ivory, his tusks weighing in at about sixty pounds apiece. He cost us one elephant hunting license and a few gray hairs. But this is why hunting in Africa is so fascinating. You never know from one moment to the next what is going to happen.

We never did see those two buffaloes again. They must have been so shocked that they left that section of the country permanently. But at any rate, be sure to include the Cape buffalo on your list of hunting "musts." No animal is a greater challenger. And remember, don't underestimate him. He never underestimates you.

CHAPTER VIII

BIRDS, BEASTS AND REPTILES

I am often asked why hippopotamuses, or "hippos," are not included in the list of dangerous game. Some people seem to think they are mean, dangerous creatures whose sole purpose in existence is to destroy native canoes, devour the occupants, and make life generally unbearable for anyone in the area. A good deal of the misbegotten impression stems from Hollywood and, like other celluloid notions, bears closer examination.

Hippos rarely cause African villages harm and never attack without good reason. (This statement applies to all wild game except the disgruntled rhino.) True, there are cases in which hippos kill natives, but usually the natives have first attacked the hippo. Some native tribes living near rivers or lakes take great delight in hunting hippo for meat. These are the same natives who complain that hippos have killed their fellow tribesmen and destroyed their villages.

The hippo, or "river horse" as he is known in Africa, is never far from water. The sun cracks his skin, making sores so deep that they afflict the animal cruelly unless he keeps his hide moist all the time. Mud baths are a special treat to hippos,

113

the coolness of the mud feeling much the same as a skin lotion feels to us. These "river horses" generally stay under water a minute or so, then come up for breath; but they have been known to stay underwater for as long as four minutes. The necessity of being in water and submerged leaves the hippo almost no defense against the hunter. When they come up for air, they make an easy shot. Even if the body submerges, it will rise in a matter of hours, the gases that quickly accumulate pushing it to the top, so that the animal can be retrieved without difficulty.

As far as I'm concerned, this type of hunting is not a sport. Hippos mind their own business and are peaceful creatures by nature. I have never understood why people insist on killing them. They are not trophies, and I can't remember when a safari client has asked the cook to serve a hippo steak.

Hippos feed at night when the sun no longer can hurt their hides. They give an appearance of being lazy, but this is deceptive. They have been known to walk for miles to secure the sweet grasses and plants growing along the riverbank.

Since safaris camp near water whenever possible, it is not unusual to have hippos as nightly visitors. They are curious animals and I am sure they come around for company. I have never actually seen them enter camp while the fires were burning high and the kerosene lamps were lit, but their nearby grunts tell the camp they are happily engaged as observers. When camp is asleep, the hippo gathers his courage for a closer look. It is not unusual to find tracks right outside your tent. But I have never heard of them causing harm to a safari party.

If you want to shoot a hippo—and I can't imagine why unless to feed the local tribe—you will have no difficulty getting one. If the animal is resting on a sand or mud flat, the brain shot is simple, and it is easy to retrieve the body.

One important thing to remember around hippos is never to get between the animal and water. Although the "river horse" is normally a peaceable creature, he feels a sense of panic when he thinks any human or animal is separating him from the safety of water. Hippos have an amazing speed and are not afraid to charge anything that blocks the way to safety. If his feet do not trample you, his jaws will make an unpleasant end to your safari.

While I am speaking of water, I will mention a few words about crocodiles. These reptiles give me an uneasy feeling every time I am around them—and they cause a high number of deaths to Africans each year, which makes them bitterly feared by the natives.

The crocodile's favorite pastime is to sun himself on a mud flat by the river's edge. He seems as rigid as a stone statue when you first observe him; but if you take a swim, that statue will turn into a thrashing devil. I have seen crocodiles gallop along a riverbank with a lightning speed and hurl themselves upon a victim before he realized what was happening.

The crocodile's jaws contain row upon row of wicked teeth. But these are not, oddly enough, the biggest danger. The tail is the most deadly weapon, and can be used to great advantage in an attack. The force of the crocodile's tail can smash a canoe or crush a man senseless with one blow.

A crocodile's favorite trick is to hide quietly under moss or other vegetation lapping over the riverbank, with only his snout above water for breathing purposes. Should an animal come down to drink, or a native approach the river's edge, the crocodile leaps into action. Nobody knows how many animals

115

are devoured by crocodiles each year; and the count of natives is uncertain, but the total figure is fantastically high.

The crocodile kills his victim by drowning. Because the jaws do not chew well, the reptile prefers to drag his kill down to the bottom of the river bed and bury it. After a week or two, the victim is rotten enough so that the crocodile has no difficulty devouring the flesh.

Crocodiles' favorite food, besides man, is fish, antelope, and cattle. Fish and game wardens say it is impossible to guess how many fish are killed each year in Africa's rivers and lakes. This presents a problem of survival for the African. Many tribes living near water rely on fish as their principal sustenance. Also, the fish these natives do not eat are traded for other food with tribes farther inland.

If you ever get the chance to hunt crocodile, the best shot for an instant kill is through the ear and into the brain. When he is in water, shoot slightly above and between the eyes. Some Africans hunt these reptiles with clubs. This is extraordinarily dangerous and always amazes me when I hear about it. One end of the weapon is tipped with heavy metal. The native sneaks up behind the drowsing crocodile and gives him a smashing blow in the center of the skull. Should the African miss, the crocodile will see how good his aim is with his thrashing tail and massive jaw.

There are native tribes that have huge hooks with which to catch crocodiles, drowning them while the reptiles struggle for freedom. I have always considered this a far more sensible way in which to enter the leather business.

One of my favorite animals is the giraffe. It is the tallest of Africa's game species and has tremendous speed. Giraffes grow as high as twenty feet, have small short horns covered with skin and hair, and live chiefly on acacia and mimosa leaves. Their tongues are quite extensive, and their lips very mobile. Like the camel, they can go for long periods of time without water. The hide, which is beautifully patterned, is an inch thick, very tough and very durable. For this reason, it is highly esteemed.

In the early times of settling Kenya, many giraffes were so wantonly slaughtered that today the animal is protected by game laws and is known as the Royal Game. Only by special permission of the royal family, or by special permission from the residing governors of Kenya and Tanganyika, may you kill one. Museum collectors are about the only people given that permission.

These long-legged animals apppear to trot in slow motion, but they cover tremendous distances with their huge strides. Their hind legs are also dangerous weapons, and their powerful kick has turned away many a lion. Giraffes seem to know, today, that they are protected, for they are losing their famed shyness and it is easy now to approach large herds on foot.

British East Africa has two species of zebra, Grévy's zebra and the common zebra. The Grévy is the more beautiful, with a larger body and narrower stripes. However, he is found only in the Northern Frontier District of Kenya. His cousin, the common zebra, is found throughout all of Kenya and Tanganyika.

Zebras run with herds of other plains game and have the annoying habit of spooking animals you may be stalking in the same area. Their eyesight is excellent, as is their scent and hearing. While the herd is grazing, there are always a few alert stallions acting as sentries for the others. Zebra skin is much in demand by sportsmen, who choose this skin above all others to decorate their trophy rooms and dens. Professional hunters have quite another use for this animal. A zebra makes the finest kind of lion bait.

There are many species of antelope in Africa. (There is an Asian variety as well.) I shall discuss only the more interesting varieties, though the sportsman finds them all a challenge during safari.

The impala antelope travel in great herds and are found in plentiful numbers in many parts of Kenya and Tanganyika. One of the greatest sights is that of the impala leaping straight up into the air when something has frightened them. They bound off in all directions, hurtling to heights as much as six feet at a time.

Impala are extremely cautious, for they never know when the leopard or cheetah is in a nearby tree or bush awaiting a meal. Their skin is beautifully soft and much in demand for coverings for wallets, purses, furniture, and so on. The impala is also a favorite of most camp cooks; there are few animals which offer more tender steaks and chops.

The Thompson gazelle stands approximately two feet high and is seen in greater numbers than any other animal in Kenya and Tanganyika. These harmless little creatures dot the plains by the thousands and offer Africa's visitors hours of enjoyment watching them playfully skip around. Leopards, lions, and cheetahs rarely choose "tommies" as a meal, for they hardly make a mouthful. Again the camp cook proves to be a bigger menace, because no meat (except eland) is more succulent.

The eland is Africa's largest antelope. The big males, or bulls, weigh well over a thousand pounds and present a magnificent sight, with their great horns twisting upward in spirals. The mature bulls are a dark grayish black. The older ones often prefer to remain alone and rarely venture out from thick underbrush. The young herd bulls act as sentinels for the lighter-colored females, seeing that the herd is never too far from cover.

The eland is suspicious by nature and can cover short distances with great speed when he is on guard. Once you shoot and miss, you can't expect to get another chance at that group. Eland meat tastes like baby beef and is a favorite course on safari. Poachers (Africans who hunt game illegally) are in constant search for eland. Local villages pay a high price for the meat.

Each year many hunters miss bagging an eland because they underestimate the animal's strength and stamina. The hunter uses the same light-caliber rifle as he would on smaller antelope and gazelle, and it is always the same story. After firing three or four shots, these inexperienced hunters wonder why the eland hardly falters as he crashes into cover. I advise you to use a .375 Magnum and not be ashamed of your weapon.

The animal's resistance is tremendous and you must have that much heavy shock power to knock him down. An experience of mine with eland, told in a following chapter, emphasizes this point.

The roan antelope has the distinction of being the second largest member of the antelope family. This big, stately animal with curving, swept-back horns, prefers to remain in thick cover and rarely do you see them out in the open. Therefore, in order to get your trophy, you may have to walk many miles, tracking in heavy forest areas. The roan antelope is so scarce in Kenya that he is completely protected by game conservation laws. You will have to visit Tanganyika to get your roan, where the animal has managed to survive in larger numbers.

There are two species of waterbuck in British East Africa, the common waterbuck and the larger defasso waterbuck. They are rarely away from water and a person generally travels along the rivers when hunting these animals. There is no special time of day they come out of the thick cover of forests and underbrush. I know that I have never been able to figure out their individual habits. I have come across a herd of waterbuck and when the animals spotted me at a distance, they were off in a split second, crashing through underbrush. In the same day, I saw a herd of fifteen waterbuck who stared at me with curiosity and finally ambled off, after I approached them within fifteen yards. They make good bait for lion and leopard, but their meat is too tough for human consumption.

The greater kudu, a member of the antelope family, is certainly one of Africa's finest trophies. At one time, this animal roamed throughout Africa in great numbers, but it is now becoming something of a rarity. Some greater kudu are found in Kenya's Northern Frontier District, but they mostly live in Tanganyika. Rinderpest's disease has drastically reduced the numbers of this much-sought-after animal.

He is shy, alert, and gravely suspicious. Greater kudu prefer to live on the tops of mountains and in thickly wooded areas. It is not wise to hunt in greater-kudu country in a car; for at the first sound of the engine, these antelope disappear into cover. Your own silence is your greatest weapon when you are matching wits with the greater kudu.

This means following up tracks mile after mile, making sure the wind will not carry your scent and alarm the animal. And you must be extremely careful how you place your feet as you track, so that you do not even step on a dry twig. You will not get much more than a fast shot even when you take your greater kudu by surprise.

Very early in the morning or in the late afternoon, the greater kudu will sometimes come out to feed around the fringe areas of the brush and forests where he takes cover all day. Occasionally he may have to cross an open stretch of ground when going to drink at a nearby river or stream. Many professional hunters prefer to take their clients to a high spot looking over an area where kudu are known to be. Client and hunter will sit there quietly all day scanning the bush and forest fringes with powerful binoculars. Then, if they are extremely fortunate, the greater kudu will come out of cover. The only other way to hunt greater kudu is the slow and tedious process of stalking them in thick cover. Sometimes the sportsman is lucky enough to take the antelope by surprise. Most times, he will hear but never see this elusive animal. But, as your professional white hunter will tell you from the start: "Make sure that first shot counts, because it is hardly likely that you will get another."

The greater kudu is an animal I discreetly leave out of my discussions on hunting. I have never shot one, but I have shot at many. I might go so far as to say when greater kudu know I am in the area, they pass the word around that all is safe. Why I repeatedly miss this big target is something that fellow hunters, my gunbearer, and particularly myself cannot understand. All someone has to do is say "greater kudu" and I react like a child during his first haircut. I completely fall apart and proceed to overshoot, undershoot, jerk the trigger, trip over logs and do anything else which would virtually destroy my chances of ending up with this magnificent trophy. As I write these words, one of Africa's greatest hunters, Eric

Rundgren, is making preparations for a little jaunt we pro-
pose to take for the specific and sole purpose of finding a deaf,
dumb, and blind greater kudu. If there is one in Africa, Eric
will find him and I shall make my approach with sneakers and
cannon.

The lesser kudu are no less evasive than their larger fellows.
Although they are more plentiful in Kenya and Tanganyika,
they are still very difficult to hunt, as they blend in perfectly
with dry bush country. The lesser kudu do not move a
muscle when danger approaches and only the trained eye can
spot them camouflaged in the natural background around
them.

Generally speaking, it is wise to track these animals. Their
one downfall, unlike their cousins, is their natural curiosity.
Once the greater kudu is spooked, he is off and running for a
long time; but the lesser kudu's curiosity oftentimes causes
him to stop and turn around for a few moments to see what
has frightened him. This is when you take your shot. I might
add, no lesser kudu is so curious that he pauses after he has
been shot at. So take excellent aim, and you will have a trophy
well worth being proud of.

In my opinion there is no animal in Africa more beautiful
than the sable antelope. The few in Kenya are protected, but
one can hunt them in Tanganyika. The male is black with a
white stomach and his thick horns sweep back over his body
in an impressive symmetry. I confess a certain amount of
pride when I talk about this magnificent trophy, and at the
risk of being immodest, I must report that I recently shot a
sable antelope standing as Number 3 in the world record book
for Tanganyika sable antelope. This gallant old fellow's horns
measured forty-six and one-half inches.

There is one drawback to hunting the sable antelope, the

122

greater kudu, and the roan antelope. They live in tsetse fly country. The tsetse fly is a horrible little monster whose bite is as painful as a bee sting and which lives off blood—whether it is yours or an animal's. It would not be too bad if these flies did not travel in squadrons. It is not unusual for the sportsman to come in from a day's hunt covered with welts and swearing that no animal is worth such discomfort. After two or three days' hunting in these fly areas, you either become a dedicated hunter and remain, or you forget a particular trophy and move camp to a saner area for other game.

Your only weapon for the tsetse fly is patience and forbearance. If you swat, swat with a vengeance. Unless the tsetse has been absolutely crushed, he will remain in a state of semiconsciousness for a moment or two and then come at you with a desire for revenge you could not have believed possible. Wear a long-sleeved khaki shirt, wrap a light scarf around your neck, and secure tightly your trouser cuffs. This will leave only your face and hands to feast on.

The bongo antelope is the sportsman's greatest challenge in Africa. The bongo is large in size and extremely shy in disposition. He is a creature of the forest and rarely strays from his protection there. He can be found in Kenya's Aberdar Kenangop range and the Mau forests. It is not unusual for sportsmen to spend years hunting one and meet with failure. The bongo is a "one-shot" animal.

The gerenuk or Waller's gazelle lives in the semidesert regions of Kenya and Tanganyika and they are particularly plentiful in the northern regions of Kenya. Because of this animal's long neck, he is sometimes referred to as the "giraffe antelope." I am always amused when I see a gerenuk standing on his hind feet while feeding on leaves from high tree limbs. They remain in this unusual position for minutes at a time.

This is not an easy trophy to hunt, for the shy gerenuk seldom strays from cover.

The wildebeest roams the plains by the thousands in Kenya and Tanganyika. It is the ugliest member of the antelope family and the most stupid. A wildebeest resembles the American buffalo in size and horn, but certainly not in spirit. The wildebeest's entire attitude may be summed up as one of helplessness. They are easy prey for lions, leopards, and cheetahs, and even wild dog packs. When a hunter needs lion bait in a hurry, he will first look for a herd of wildebeests. They rarely stampede when they see your Land Rover, and even if they do start off, they will only go a few hundred yards before stopping.

The hartebeest is a distant cousin to the wildebeest. This antelope is commonly referred to as the kongoni. He travels the plains but is also found in thick cover. The hartebeest is sometimes confused with the topi antelope. They have much the same features from a distance, although the topi has a chocolate coloring and the hartebeest is lighter brown. The hartebeest is the fastest of all antelope. Even the cheetah has a difficult time bringing down this animal.

Speaking of cheetahs, I'd like to say a few words about these lovely spotted animals. There is in Africa no animal faster for the first few hundred yards and he can knock down most antelope with one bounding leap.

The cheetah resembles the leopard, although he is thinner and has longer claws. This animal prefers to hunt in open country. He can successfully do so because of his great speed. He is neither as graceful as the leopard nor as exclusive.

Leopards prefer to remain by themselves, while the cheetah favors company. I have seen groups of these animals in threes and fours padding across the open plains in search of food. The cheetah is not vicious, and I have never heard of one attacking a man. Because his nature is friendly and tame, game authorities have outlawed the shooting of the cheetah. These protected animals have been known to make fine pets and many of Africa's visitors have brought them home for exactly this reason.

The bushbuck and reedbuck are cousins. Both species travel in couples. The bushbuck's dark coloring is particularly beautiful. He chooses to live in the type of country his name implies, thick bush country. Only the males have horns in the bushbuck and the reedbuck species. The reedbuck is not quite as shy as his cousin. You are apt to find him near streams and rivers. They are shy, gentle, little animals and their curiosity oftentimes is their downfall. When approached by hunters, reedbucks will stand right where they are, bounding off only at the last minute. They should take a lesson from the bushbuck, who rarely offers so fine a target.

The Grant's gazelle can be found in numerous numbers in Kenya and Tanganyika. They are strictly plains-game animals and thrive in dry bush country. The Grant's gazelle is one of the few animals who can survive without water, doing quite well with the moisture they get while feeding. His greatest enemy is the cheetah and leopard. His meat is indigestible and I have seen hungry Africans turn down this gazelle for supper. Once I chewed on a Grant gazelle steak for what seemed several hours, so I understand the Africans' point of view.

The klipspringer lives in rocky hill country. This tiny antelope is less than two feet tall. They are masters of camouflage. When they stand against a background of rock, it is almost impossible to see them. Bring along your mountain climbing shoes when you hunt these elusive little animals and make sure your eyes are well rested, for it requires close scrutiny to be able to pick out this trophy.

When you hunt the sitatunga, a member of the bushbuck species, you are in for long and discouraging hours. They live in swamps and marshes, most of which offer the sitatunga perfect protection from man. Most times, a hunter will have to wait patiently day after day in concealed cover, while hoping a sitatunga will appear in his line of fire. They rarely move about in the day, preferring to feed at night. When frightened, they have been known to submerge themselves completely in water with just their snouts sticking out for air. This is an animal which, like the bongo, challenges the imagination and determination of the sportsman. I know of hunters who have devoted their entire safari to hunting the sitatunga. They have still to see one.

The ostrich is the largest bird in the world. The male has beautiful plumage of black and white, in striking contrast to the female's dull brownish feathers. The female ostrich lays eggs and hatches her young in the same manner as the barnyard chicken, although the male ostrich is more considerate than the rooster, for he takes turns with his mate, sitting on top of the nest to give the eggs warmth.

The ostrich is one of the greatest actors of all time. If you approach either the male or female sitting on top of the nest, this bird will limp off in a direction away from the eggs, pretending to be sick or hurt. The ostrich hopes the intruder will give pursuit and thus stay away from the nest. Personally, I am always delighted whenever their Academy Award performance fools man or animal.

This giant bird does not fly, and it gives a rather odd, plucked appearance around the head, neck and thighs, where there are few feathers. It can run extremely fast and for great distances. Many a hunter has been fooled when the ostriches ruffle their plumage, especially around their chests, so that it protruded to such an extent that the bullets zipped through the feathers.

Ostrich feathers were—and are—considered great prizes for the use of decoration, but their importation to America is now outlawed. Africans are particularly fond of the male's black and white plummage. I know certain safari camp boys whom I could entrust with any amount of money, but they'd "steal" a few feathers if given the chance.

I think the question "Will we see any snakes on our safari?" is asked more often than any other by clients when they first meet their white hunter. If a client is apt to be very nervous and excitable, the hunter may tactfully reply, "I've been hunting in Africa for twenty years and I've seen very few." Of course this is a white lie, but generally said to reassure, so it can perhaps be overlooked. The truth of the matter is that if you go on safari, you have an excellent chance of coming within throwing distance of a poisonous reptile.

Certainly the most dangerous snake in British East Africa is the Gaboon viper. This reptile can grow to be six feet long and has a body thicker than a man's leg. Death comes almost instantaneously from the Gaboon viper's bite, and unless you give immediate medical attention to the victim, the person dies in two to five minutes.

A well-known snake in Africa is the python. These snakes have been known to achieve eighteen feet in length. Although a python's bite is not poisonous, the damage it can do can be as fatal as a bite from the deadly mamba. The python wraps its coils around its victim and squeezes it to death. Once this has been accomplished, the snake attempts to devour the crushed remains. Pythons have been known to have fights with lions, leopards, and Cape buffaloes, and to have bested their opponents.

There are many nonpoisonous snakes in Africa, but the rule of thumb I go by is, don't wait to find out.

One of the greatest gifts medicine has provided for the safari-goer, the settler, and the African is the Fitzsimmons snake serum outfit. No one should hunt in Africa without having a kit with him at all times, and I strongly suggest reading the book of directions thoroughly before setting out for your first day in the bush. The Fitzsimmons directions are easy to understand, and they give you complete directions and descriptions concerning all reptiles found in Africa.

Although the subject of snake bites is disagreeable, I think I should take the time to answer a question often asked of me: "What can you do to help a person bitten by a poisonous reptile?" The most important thing to remember is to tie a tourniquet above the bite if at all possible. This is done when a snake strikes an arm or leg. With a clean knife or razor blade, make a deep crosscross cut through each fang wound and rub in permanganate crystals. Then inject antivenom serum into the bite area. All this equipment comes in the Fitzsimmons snake kit. Try not to move the person who has been bitten and keep the patient quiet and warm. Remember, shock can be as deadly as venom.

When a bite occurs on the body or face, applying a tourniquet is impossible. This is why the injection of serum immediately in the afflicted area is so important. The emergency application is the same regardless what poisonous snake bites you, only the quantity of serum differs.

Snakes, in most cases, are as anxious to get out of your way as you are to get out of theirs. The accidents that do happen are those that are just what you suspect—when someone crosses a snake's path as the snake is trying to seek safety, or when someone steps on a snake resting in bush cover. Most snakes will give you warning, either by rearing up and letting you see them, or by making a hissing noise.

During a recent safari, one of our hunting party let out a shriek one evening as he came tearing out of the camp stall shower. He found he was sharing his evening bath with a puff adder. The snake had been thirsty, apparently.

I cannot forget an unpleasant incident that happened on safari several years ago. In our mess tent, we had a butane gas refrigerator. One day our entire hunting party was sitting around the dining table waiting for dinner. The Number One head boy, Matiso, opened the refrigerator door to get some butter for the table.

The next thing we knew, we heard a scream and a hissing sound. The head boy stumbled back over the chairs, clutching his hands to his face. Everyone knew what had happened. A spitting cobra had squirted its venom into Matiso's eyes. On top of the refrigerator, coiled around the motor for warmth, was a fighting-mad cobra.

The snake reared up and was challenging everyone. We dragged the screaming native outside and placed him on the ground. Our four camp boys held his hands in order to stop him from rubbing more of the poison into his eyes. We poured condensed milk into the poor chap's eyes, which is about the only thing you can do to neutralize the poison, as well as relieve the pain.

Meanwhile, Arthur Crowley, a friend and great sportsman I have hunted with for years, immediately took care of the cobra with a .22 pistol. I am happy to report our head boy was back at his duties within two weeks. (A most unusual recovery.) Had it been another species of cobra whose fangs struck at the man's face, it would have been a far different story. Our head boy would have been dead in minutes.

You are bound to see snakes along the roads. Reptiles love warmth and dirt roads seem not to cool as swiftly as ground with vegetation. There is a well-traveled road leading to Nairobi where it is not unusual for a person to count as many as thirty poisonous snakes during a two-hour drive. I would take particular care when leaving a road and going cross country by foot. I believe I have seen more poisonous reptiles curled up in cover by a road's edge than in any other specific terrain.

In conclusion, let me say this. The chances of your being bitten by a snake are just about nil. You will probably see snakes, poisonous and nonpoisonous, on your safari, but very few people like to challenge a snake, and the snake feels the same way. (Frankly, you're more apt to end up as a casualty from slipping off a bar stool during a "breather" in Nairobi!)

CHAPTER IX

STARTING A SAFARI

I know of no true sportsman who has not longed to shoot the Big Five, and any man who has been in the bush has only one thought in mind: When can he return to Africa?

Provided you have the necessary capital—or think you will be able to scrape it together, which is the same thing—you begin by contacting a safari agency to make the arrangements for your trip. There are several outstanding ones in Nairobi: Ker and Downey, the White Hunters (Africa) Ltd., Safariland, Ltd., Selby and Holmberg, Tanganyika Guides and Tours, to mention a few of the more famous ones, who will advise you on all the perplexities that arise and will comfort you in your pre-safari worries. Almost assuredly, there will be very few adversities. Safari outfitters take *very* good care of their clients.

In your letter you will want to provide the following information:

1. The estimated day of your arrival and where you will be coming in, either at the airport in Nairobi, or by sea in

Mombasa, the port for Kenya, some hundred fifty miles away.

2. The length of time you expect to spend on safari and the total number of persons in your party (including age, sex, relationship, etc.).

3. List of the type of game you are particularly anxious to hunt.

4. Lastly, and most important, be sure to specify whether you want a photographic or hunting safari, or both.

The price quoted to you by the firm will include everything necessary in the field and the best modern equipment, excluding guns, cost of game licenses, ammunition, photographic equipment, cigarettes and alcoholic beverages, and personal expenses such as clothing and tipping.

What the safari firm provides, however, makes an impressive list:

1. The professional white hunter.

2. Full tentage, including dining tent, double-fly sleeping tents with bath area and veranda attached, lavatory tents, and the African staff to service these.

3. Full camp equipment, including beds, tables, chairs, mosquito netting, linen, lamps, water filters, cutlery, cooking utensils, radio receiving set, portable canvas bathtubs, shower equipment.

4. African staff, gunbearers, skinners, drivers, cooks, personal servants, waiters and porters.

5. Food and soft drinks for the party on a scale that is more than generous. There is a tempting list of canned foods available which will be shown to you before leaving, for your approval. Fresh meats and vegetables are acquired

regularly "in the field." Special foods for diets can be ordered in advance.

6. Medicine kit and first-aid chest.
7. A safari hunting car is supplied with every professional white hunter (the white hunter never takes care of more than two clients). One five-ton truck to transport tents, camp equipment, African staff, trophies, for parties of one or two clients. (Two trucks are necessary for every two persons.) For one month's safari, a free mileage allowance of 1,500 miles for each hunting car and a little less for each lorry.
8. Hotel accommodation charges during safari, but not in Nairobi.
9. Treatment and preservation of trophies during the safari, but you must pay for your own dipping, packing, and shipment.

While certainly all of the essentials and most of the luxuries for a pleasant trip are included, the charge does not provide for a refrigerator or for electric lighting, unless you make a special request for these, and then there is a nominal charge.

You may have your own guns, you may want to purchase them, or perhaps you will rent them. Heavy double-barreled rifles can be hired for about thirty to thirty-five dollars a month; light and medium rifles are a little less. The game laws forbid the use of a rifle of less than .375 for the lion and eland. A .400 is the smallest bore permitted for shooting elephant, rhino, buffalo, and hippo. The use of a .22 L.R. or a .22 W.R.F. is not allowed for game animals, but may be used for birds and target practice.

If you are taking your own guns, I suggest that if you go by air, you ship them ahead by sea. Allow at least four months before the starting date of your safari for shipment. Most clients ask their safari outfitter to purchase ammunition; however, supplies and types are sometimes limited, and it is wise to advise your safari agent well in advance what caliber rifles you intend to use.

NOTE: When your safari is at last confirmed, the agency will send you a Firearm Certificate Application, and you must fill in all the makes and calibers of weapons, with their serial numbers, together with the amount and calibers of ammunition that you intend to bring. Once these forms have been turned in, no change can be made without great difficulty.

You need a passport, and should have visas for Kenya, Tanganyika, and Uganda; you get these by applying to the British Consul. You should send the *full* names of your party so that the agency can obtain the permits and meet you, with them, on your arrival. The Immigration Authorities require a certificate of vaccination against smallpox and a certificate of inoculation against yellow fever. Use the international form. Your safari medicine kit will carry protection against malaria. Write your safari agent about other shots you may need. It all depends on the area you will hunt.

Camera and binoculars are taken through customs easiest if you take them yourself, instead of sending them in advance. You will not have to pay a staggering customs duty on each if you carry them on your person. Film must be declared, and is usually sent on ahead of the client because of weight and bulk. However, film may be purchased in Nairobi.

Most safari agencies recommend that you travel by air for speed, comfort, and convenience. There is a direct service from the United States ports by sea via South Africa to Mombasa, if you prefer a leisurely cruise. The trip takes approximately six weeks.

The American-South African and Robin Lines have a limited number of excellent first-class passages for the sea route, and they operate a fortnightly service on their fast cargo steamers. Airlines that operate in and out of Nairobi are: B.O.A.C. (British Overseas Airways Corp.), S.A.S. (Scandinavian Airlines System), South African Airways, Air France, and Italian Air Lines. Air service is uniformly excellent.

Of course, the problem of outfitting yourself will be foremost in your mind. The following clothing is recommended for men by safari outfitters. I would also like to add that you can have your actual hunting clothing made in Nairobi, where khaki bush jackets with cartridge holders sewn on and khaki slacks are tailored by hand in twenty-four hours. Safari outfitters will send you a measurement form to fill out in advance so the initial tailoring job can be completed at the time of your arrival.

2 khaki drill bush shirts and trousers
3 khaki shirts
1 pair mosquito boots (not essential)
1 pair tennis sneakers
1 terai hat (purchase this in Nairobi)
1 raincoat (I suggest the light plastic type)
2 pairs light but strong ankle-height walking boots
2 pairs shoes for camp wear
    thick woolen socks
    underwear
1 pullover, neutral-colored
    handkerchiefs
2 pairs pajamas

2 pairs sunglasses
toilet articles
1 binoculars, 7 x 50 or 8 x 30

Your safari trunk, a tin trunk you can also purchase in Nai-robi, is a must. And I would suggest one or two summer suits for your stay in the capital.

I suggest the following "unofficial equipment," not listed by the outfitters as essential, but which has proven most essential to me:

1 heavy sweater—turtle-neck style
1 light sweater—feels wonderful during the early morning chill
1 terry-cloth bathrobe—for after that hot bath or shower
lip chapsticks—that sun is hot
plastic bags for camera equipment—keep out the dust
a light scarf—great neck protection from the sun and tsetse fly
several cravats—more comfortable than ties when in Nairobi (An open shirt and cravat is most acceptable in hotels and clubs.)
plastic rifle bags—keep out the dirt
pencil flashlight—a safety measure in camp or while traveling at night
a whistle—another excellent safety measure should you get lost
a compass—you'll need it!
optical cleaning tissues—for eyeglasses and binoculars
plastic flask—there will be times you'll want it!

2 terry-cloth jump suits—wonderful for lounging
woolly slippers—best friend your tired feet ever had

1 small icebucket—a cold thirst quencher in the middle
of the day is a lifesaver

1 pair of light leather gloves—great for traveling
through thorny terrain when you're not actually
hunting

1 light canvas carrying case—it carries all the things
normally stuffed into pockets, cigarettes, extra
socks, extra pair sunglasses, ammunition

1 Zippo lighter—matches are a nuisance (Don't forget
extra flints and lighter fluid.)

1 skinning knife and sheath—you can help the boys
skin your trophies

1 jackknife—the type with following attachments:
corkscrew, bottle opener, can opener, punch, tweez-
ers, screwdriver, blades

1 wrist watch—shockproof, antimagnetic, waterproof,
with strong leather band

1 portable writing pad set and ball-point pens—con-
ventional type of ink fountain pen is messy because
of heat

1 pistol belt—for sunglass holder, knife, leather cartridge holders

1 plastic cigarette case—a container shaped to hold a
cigarette package; keeps out dust and rain, prevents
cigarettes from crumbling
leather cartridge holders—slip on belt and you won't
have to fumble around pockets for ammo

1 Polaroid camera and film—nothing delights Africans
more than an instantaneous picture of themselves;
excellent for trading trinkets

Women follow more or less the same style as men, avoiding all bright colors when they are in the bush. The wardrobe should include a few khaki skirts—but no shorts, please. Shoes may be of the brogue variety, with rubber soles. Since nights are cool, bring a couple of jerseys and a warm jacket. I'm not really too much up on women's creams, but other women who have been on safari tell me I should advise you to stock up. You'll use them.

A competent photographer to accompany the safari may also be hired. (He supplies his own camera car.) Rates vary, but in general he will receive about twenty-five dollars a day if you provide the cameras, more if he supplies his own. Many hunting safaris use professional photographers to record their shooting exploits on film.

Unless you are particularly hearty and rain doesn't dampen your enthusiasm or determination, most safari organizers agree that the best time of year to make your trip is between rainy spells, which usually commence about the first of April and end the beginning of June—May being the worst month. This applies to the best hunting districts in Kenya and Tanganyika; in Southern Tanganyika, the rains commence the end of October and continue until about the first of June.

From July to November are the best hunting months.

However, there is no closed season on game, and you can hunt during wet weather if you don't take to heart the swollen rivers, the soggy marshes, and the soft mud flats; and you will discover that tracking in wet season is a good deal easier than in dry.

Most of your shooting, with the exception of elephant, takes place at altitudes of 4,000 to 5,000 feet. There is little variation during the seasons, the temperature ranging from 70° to 80°.

Although Kenya straddles the equator, contrary to what you would assume, it is *not* extremely hot. Nights are chilly and the early morning hours, when most of your hunting is done, are downright cold. The temperature often falls to 40° in the course of the night.

The jungle comes alive at night. Some animals attempt light sleep while Africa's carnivorous species of wild game go on the prowl to appease their hunger pangs. Night is not welcomed by animals who must be constantly alert for the leopard, lion and cheetah, or the treacherous wild dog packs and the patient hyena.

After sundown, Africa's soft-skin animals, such as impala, topi, wildebeest, hartebeest, oryx, Thomson's and Grant's gazelle, giraffe, and zebra appear. There is little unprovoked motion, for movement attracts attention.

Darkness serves the needs of other animals as well. Africa's thick-skinned animals, such as rhino, buffalo, hippo, and elephant, unmolested by scorching sun, leisurely feed and water at night, undisturbed by man with his spear, bow and arrow, and gun.

So while safari camp members are fast asleep, Africa's forests and rolling plains unfold in tense activity.

Be prepared to rise early on safari. Animals, like most sensible people, take cover from the scorching, tropical sun. The midday heat is unrelenting, and Africa's game seeks shade wherever possible. Little cover is found on the plains, so animals identified with this open terrain simply lie down and remain motionless. Therefore, the sportsman must be properly located in the area he wishes to hunt while animals still elect to travel during early morning. The majority of game is spotted between sunup and 10:00 A.M., and from 3:00 P.M. to sundown.

Once your hunting day commences and you leave camp, you rarely will return until evening. Lunch is prepared thoughtfully by the camp cook and placed in your hunting car's chop box.

People are invariably surprised at how little they eat during a day. Perhaps it's the fact that they eat a heartier breakfast than they do at home. Also Africa's sun has a sapping effect on one's strength and appetite. A tin of lobster or a cold partridge suffices my tastes. There will be many times when food is the last thing in your mind, particularly when on the fresh trail of a worth-while trophy.

The end of the day, when last shooting light melts into dusk, you head back to the most welcome sight in the world —your safari campfire.

The three areas I prefer to hunt most in British East Africa are the Northern Frontier District in Kenya Colony, the Narok area in Kenya's Northern Masailand, and the Rungwa area in Southern Tanganyika.

One last tip before you get under way. I would strongly recommend that you have your bank transfer some money to the Standard Bank of South Africa, Nairobi; enough to cover the expenses of the safari and your other costs while you are in British East Africa. Traveler's checks are quite satisfactory, if you don't mind the high commission for changing them. Should you have any money left over, it can readily be transferred back to your original bank account.

CHAPTER X

GUNS

Kenya firearms laws allow the hunter to bring five firearms and a specified quantity of ammunition into the colony. No semiautomatic or pump firearms are allowed. This simply means that your rifles—both center and rim fire—and shotguns must be either bolt action, lever action or double-barreled. Since lever actions are usually chambered for either obsolete or impractical cartridges for African game, we can consider this to mean bolt-actions and double-barreled firearms.

The most important section of an African arsenal is the center-fire group. Since most hunters are concerned with the big game when they come to Africa, the center-fire rifles should receive special attention. There is a wide variety of big game in Africa so that there is necessity for more than one big-game center-fire rifle. Actually, the prospective African hunter should plan to allot three berths for center-fires in his limit of five firearms. These should be a heavy bore for the biggest game (elephant, buffalo, rhino), a medium bore for intermediate game (lion, eland), a small bore for plains shooting (for the various antelopes).

Game laws specify that rifles of not less than .400 caliber may be used on the "top three"—elephant, buffalo, or rhino. Hence, this eliminates calibers like the .375 Magnum although they may have been used effectively in the past. When one considers that the average man on safari is there for one time in his life, this is a very sensible law. After all, the majority of "first-timers" on safari are unfamiliar with dangerous game and need all the punch they can carry. There are a number of rifles, both bolt action and double, that provide all that is needed for the biggest and most dangerous game in the world.

Although there are some giant rifles made by the English in the range of the .577 and .600 Nitro Express, the Safari enthusiast is best served by those in the .400-caliber area. In the first place, the sensation of shooting a .600 can only be compared to being hit by an express train. Secondly, and most importantly, the .400s do the job quite adequately. Favored double-barreled rifles are those made by various English gunmakers for the .470 and .465 Nitro Express. For those who prefer English bolt-action magazine rifles, there are the .416 Rigby and the .425 Westley Richards. If a little more gun is desired, the .505 Gibbs is made in bolt action as well.

All of the above big rifles are of English origin and most rifles chambered in the big calibers are English. Since the British are the pioneers of African big-game hunting and still control Africa's choicest game fields, it is only natural that they should have been the leaders in developing African rifles and loads. However, there are a number of foreign actions made for the various large English calibers. Certain European double rifles are manufactured and Mauser actions are available for the big cartridges.

Perhaps the biggest challenge to the old English supremacy

has been in the recent entry of the Winchester .458 and—to a lesser degree—the Weatherby .460. The .458 Magnum is chambered in the Winchester Model 70 rifle and is offered for quite a bit less than the English doubles and bolt-actions. The .458 is loaded with 500- and 510-grain bullets and boasts a little more than 5,000 foot-pounds of energy. Since its ballistics are practically the same as the English .470 Nitro Express—traditionally, the old-time favorite of Africa's hunters —it is perfectly suited to Africa's biggest game.

It is entirely possible the person on safari will not want to purchase a rifle he may only use one time in his life. If this is the case, the hunter can rent one of the big bores from his safari outfitter for a nominal fee, approximately forty-two dollars per month. Most outfitters carry the calibers and rifles mentioned above as well as intermediate and smaller calibers. Actually, it is possible for the hunter to rent his entire battery of firearms after he arrives in Africa, and thus avoid the bother of bringing his own.

However, before you purchase or rent your heavy-duty weapon, please consider the following. I would discourage a person with relatively little big-game hunting experience to go after the Cape buffalo, rhino, and elephant with a bolt-action rifle. In my humble opinion, this type of weapon can prove to be dangerous when hunting dangerous game if not handled by a safari veteran.

My preference is the .470 Nitro Express double-barreled rifle. The weight of bullet is 500 grains, the pressure 14.0 tons per square inch, and at a hundred yards the muzzle velocity is 2,125 feet per second. The energy in feet and pounds is 5,030 at 100 yards. These statistics add up to one thing—the .470 can stop any living animal you will encounter any place in the world.

Whenever I enter discussions regarding calibers of rifles, I pose the same question, "Why take the chance and use a caliber just within the law?" There is no room for error when hunting the Cape buffalo, rhino, and elephant. When you are the recipient of their charge, only one of you walks away.

Is it worth the chance to use a lighter-caliber rifle so you can brag about your accomplishments in the seclusion of a bar or trophy room? Certainly, hunters and clients alike have successfully dispatched these three charging animals with a lighter-caliber rifle than the .470. In fact, the .270 will kill an elephant instantly with the fatal brain shot; but the chances of the hunter getting into the proper position are extremely unlikely.

Something happens to both man and beast during a charge. In such a keyed-up situation, the animal has a decided emotional advantage. He loses all fear and his only two feelings are hate and anger. On the other hand, and with very few exceptions, fear becomes the most predominant feeling in man's emotions—of course with varying degrees of intensity, according to the individual.

I don't believe a charging animal considers for one moment that he is probably going to be killed. Man does. Therefore, a greater margin of error exists for man than for animal. The slightest hesitation, or a trembling hand, can cause the hunter to miss his target completely. Unless stopped or turned away, the charging animal will not miss his target.

Then there is the element of surprise to be seriously considered. Although you may envision that the hunter always has the element of surprise on his side when tracking elephant, rhino or buffalo, this is an entirely wrong concept. True, a person may plan a perfect stalk after he has picked out a trophy bull elephant. He may be in the perfect position for a fatal brain or heart shot and then his plan distintegrates because he didn't see the cow elephant concealed in thick underbrush, twenty yards to the right. The new target is an enraged mother protecting her child and the hunter has only a matter of seconds to stop her murderous charge. In a position such as this, the hunter needs balance as well as an accurate snap shot. No single-barreled weapon (bolt action) can compare with the balance of a double.

Then there is the question of "sound" when hunting the big three. The metallic clicking sound of a weapon or camera has provoked unexpected charges. Obviously, bolt-action rifles are the most serious offenders. Some old-time hunters feel so strongly about "sound" that they remove the ejector spring from their double-barreled Express to ensure silent action. One cannot do this with a bolt-action rifle.

I am not an expert in the subject of firearms, but I do respect the habits of professional hunters in Africa. With the exception of the .416 Rigby (bolt action), I have found double-barreled Express rifles preferred by the vast majority of professional African game hunters.

The .470 has one other distinct advantage. If your two shots do not have fatal results, you still have a commanding advantage over the animal. The weapon has a tremendous shocking, stopping power. If your bullet hits bone instead of flesh tissue, it will stun the animal and put him temporarily out of commission, thus permitting you time for an assured kill.

So whenever you hear people scoff at the use of the heavier-caliber weapons, ask them one question: "If you were in a street fight and saw a ten-foot, six-hundred-pound man come running at you with a butcher knife, would you defend yourself with a crowbar or a kid glove?"

Although there are a number of calibers in the medium-game classification that are adequate for lion and eland, we will consider the .375 Holland & Holland Magnum only. Game laws specify the use of rifles of .375 and above for lion and eland; smaller calibers—regardless of their effectiveness—are forbidden. Since a number of new Magnum calibers—for instance the new Winchester .388 Magnum, a companion to that company's .458 African—have been developed over the past few years, it is hoped this law will be amended some time in the near future.

As a consequence, a hunter should definitely plan to take a .375 Magnum with him, as it is the only rifle that correctly fills the bill as a lion gun. The .400s are too big and are not really necessary. The .375 is a very powerful cartridge and, in the past, before present game laws went into effect, was used on elephant and buffalo as well as lion. The .375 is available in a number of English and European rifles. The Winchester Model 70 is the only commercial American firearm chambered for the regular .375 H & H. Again, the sportsman can rent his .375 when he arrives in Nairobi.

When people first go on safari, they are quite apt to underestimate the stamina of African game and, therefore, use too light a caliber or rifle. The giant eland takes a lot of killing. In fact, the topi antelope, waterbuck, hartebeest, roan antelope, sable antelope, greater kudu, wildebeest, and zebra can run for miles even though fatally wounded.

I will always remember the time on safari we needed a quantity of meat immediately because we had promised the meat to a native village as payment for photographing a dance. This particular village had expensive tastes and the African chief insisted on eland meat as the main course. Ordinarily zebra or any other of the antelope family would have been sufficient. This particular day the other rifles in my battery

146

were being used by members of the safari, and I was left with a .270. Midday, I came across a solitary bull resting beneath the shade of a cluster of trees. The eland was unaware of my presence and I was able to approach my target to within 75 yards before firing. Had I been using my .375, my first two shots would have surely brought the eland down. The eland bolted, after receiving three "fatal" shots, and I spent the next two uncomfortable hours in pursuit of this wounded animal. I finally came upon the eland lying down in tall grass. His trail told me he was bleeding profusely so when I saw his massive form settled in cover, I presumed he was too injured to move. I maneuvered for a *coup de grâce* shot and fired. To my complete amazement, the eland practically leaped to his feet and bolted off toward thicker cover. Finally, I was able to kill him with the next shot. We had great difficulty getting a vehicle near enough to the fallen eland in order to haul the meat back to camp. I had learned my lesson. If I do not have a heavy enough caliber rifle to do the job, I will stay behind and gossip with the camp crew.

A final word about the .375. Do not expect miracles at six hundred yards. Take a little extra time and care during your stalk when the .375 is your weapon. Be sure the distance is three hundred yards or less and if you don't have a trophy in one shot, then you know the blame does not lie with the weapon.

As a suggestion, put a detachable four-power scope on your .375, for there are times you will pursue game in heavy under-brush. A scope is a decided disadvantage unless there is a re-spectable clearing between you and the animal.

The safari enthusiast comes to Africa with the Big Five uppermost in his mind. These are the animals he has traveled thousands of miles to meet. A similar number of dollars have been expended for the same goal. The rifles he will use for them will be—with one exception—the ones outlined previously, the big .400s and the .375. The one exception is for the leopard. The hunter may use his .375 on leopard; but, quite likely, he will use the third representative of his center-fires. This rifle, primarily for big game, like antelope, will account for the great majority of game taken during the safari. Hence, the rifle which is probably least important in the mind of the prospective safari client is, in actuality, the most important weapon he selects for his trip. It is the firearm he will carry and shoot most. It will account for thirty heads out of the total of forty or so the average person takes. Perhaps a bit more attention might be devoted to the selection of such an important accessory.

There is a wide variety of suitable firearms in the middle range of calibers. Rifles of this range—roughly from .250 to .375—are the great majority of center-fires throughout the world. The sportsman should have no trouble in equipping himself with a suitable firearm in this range; in fact, he probably already has one in his possession.

Naturally, this rifle should be a bolt-action (although there are a few lever-actions available in suitable calibers, they are rarely found on safari). Any sturdy and dependable rifle chambered for the .270, .30-06, .308, .300 H & H, 8mm, or any of the new 7 or 6.5 Magnums, is a perfectly suited weapon for the plains game found in Africa.

Since the safari client has the .375 as a bridge between the really big bores and this smaller category, I suggest the Winchester .270 or the .300 H & H as the ideal plains-game weapon. The new Winchester .264 Magnum (again, companion caliber to the .458 and .388 Magnums) or one of the Weatherby medium Magnums also makes an effective power package for any of the African hoofed game—with the exception of the eland, which we have already discussed.

There remain two places to be filled in the safari client's battery of weapons: the shotgun and the .22 rim-fire. Many hunters believe—without reason I think—the shotgun and rim-fire have no place on the safari. Africa is a place for big-game hunting. Why bring a shotgun—worse yet, a piddling little .22-caliber rifle? The answer is obvious. Once you have been on safari, you recognize that Africa is the greatest bird-hunting paradise left in the world. Perhaps it is the greatest the world has ever seen. Literally thousands of game birds of countless species abound in the areas used by the leading safari firms.

There are no limits, no seasons. It is a shotgunner's dream. I know of one veteran hunter from the Midwest who—perhaps in memory of his youthful days of bountiful bird hunting —annually goes to hunt birds in Africa. He doesn't even bother with the big-game species; Africa is the "only decent place left to get game birds."

Bird-hunting enthusiasts will abhor this next remark, but some of Africa's best-eating game birds reach the pot, compliments of a well-placed .22 shot. I can hear the protests now —"disgraceful, unsportsmanlike, beastly." No doubt these remarks are justified any place in the world—except in Africa. Certainly, if you are in a hunting area for the sole purpose of bird shooting, leave the .22 in camp and have a first-class wing shoot with your 12-gauge shotgun. However, if you are primarily hunting big game, but would enjoy a tasty partridge or guinea fowl, bring along the .22. One blast from a shotgun can frighten animals from the immediate area. Somehow, the report from a .22 bothers neither animals nor birds.

Other than bird hunting, a shotgun can be extremely

valuable in hunting. It is highly suitable for shooting reptiles. I know I would prefer to have my 12-gauge shotgun aimed at a weaving cobra in lieu of any other weapon with the possible exception of a Sherman tank.

The shotgun is also the most effective weapon against a wounded lion or leopard whose hiding place is in thick cover and unknown to you. When either leopard or lion make their spring at close quarters, there is not time to take careful aim and fire. Many shots are fired from the hip. Quite obviously, a double blast from a shotgun has the necessary stopping power needed in such emergencies.

Remember, game laws forbid pumps or automatic (self-loading) actions, so bring a double-barreled shotgun and bolt-action .22 rim-fire.

In addition to the restrictions noted previously, British East African laws restrict the amount of ammunition that can be brought in by the sportsman. Current laws state that each shooter may bring in 250 rounds of medium and/or light center-fire ammunition (this would cover the .250 to .375 calibers approximately); 30 rounds of heavy big-bore loads (the .400s and above); 250 rounds of shotgun ammunition.

All importation of .22-caliber ammunition is forbidden, but it can be picked up easily in Nairobi. There is a customs duty of 22 per cent of the declared value of all guns and ammunition brought into the colony. This money is held for the client and he is refunded his deposit for his guns. No refund is given on ammunition. Additional ammunition is available from the outfitter or other retail sources in Nairobi. No handguns may be brought into Kenya.

CHAPTER XI

AFTER THE HUNT

When the trip is completed and the various trophies are collected for shipment, the safari client finds himself confronted with problems as complex as those encountered before his hunt. This is the time when the successful sportsman wishes he hadn't been quite so successful— at least for a few agonizing moments.

The care and mounting of trophies can be one of the most expensive items of a safari. Yet, who would dispose of this important element of the trip of a lifetime? What would a safari be without trophies to bring back memories of an exciting chase, the campfires of Africa, and the joys and heartbreaks of many days? It is an expense that will pay for itself a hundredfold in the future.

Since trophies are such an important and expensive part of the trip, potential safari clients should have some idea what individual and collective costs are for the preservation of trophies. Remember: This is not an occasional whitetail deerhead or bear rug, but a possible thirty or so heads and skins.

Actually, the sportsman should only keep trophy heads, good representative trophies of the major species. If a man can afford it, however, he can have practically everything preserved and mounted for his den. The Africans are skilled skinners and the outfitters will keep your trophies in good shape until the taxidermist can handle them.

You have several choices in taxidermy. Trophies can be mounted in Nairobi, in Europe, or in the United States. If you choose the latter, Nairobi firms will dip your heads and skins in antivermin solution and pack them for shipment to your local taxidermist. Although Nairobi firms may be somewhat cheaper, remember that the mounted trophies will still have to be shipped home.

Hence, differences in expense between Nairobi firms and local taxidermists at home about even out. When considering other factors—convenience, trouble in shipping, and possible damage in passage—many hunters think it best to have their trophies dipped in Nairobi and shipped to a taxidermist.

The leading taxidermist in America is the firm of Jonas Brothers, with offices in Mount Vernon, New York; Denver, Colorado; and Seattle, Washington. I can also recommend highly P. Zimmerman's firm in Nairobi and Rowland Ward Taxidermy firm in London. Listed below are typical prices for various African trophies, both mounted and tanned.

JONAS BROTHERS' AFRICAN TROPHY PRICE LIST

WALLHEADS:

Hunter's antelope	$ 80.00
Roan antelope	80.00
Sable antelope	$115.00–125.00
Buffalo	$165.00–175.00
Bushbuck	45.00
Dik-dik	28.50
Duiker	37.50
Eland	$115.00–125.00
Grant's gazelle	60.00

WALLHEADS: *(cont.)*

Thompson's gazelle	$45.00
Gerenuk	60.00
Gnu	80.00
Hartebeest	75.00
Hippo (OM)	500.00
Hyena (OM)	45.00
Impala	60.00
Jackal	28.50
Klipspringer	37.50
Kongoni	75.00
Greater kudu	$110.00–120.00
Lesser kudu	75.00
Lion, male	90.00
Lioness	80.00
Oribi	37.50
Oryx	30.00
Reedbuck	55.00
Rhino	$250.00–350.00
Steinbuck	37.50
Topi	75.00
Waterbuck	85.00
Wart hog	75.00
Zebra	95.00
Leopard	65.00

LIFE-SIZE MOUNTING:

Dik-dik	$ 100.00
Thompson's gazelle	250.00
Leopard	450.00
Oribi	175.00
Steinbuck	200.00
Lion, male	$750.00–1,000.00
Leopard, ½ mount	225.00

NOTE: The above prices for standard forms; higher prices apply to specially modeled forms and mountings.

Horns on Panel, Bronzing Skull, or With Leather Cover:
Buffalo horns	$ 40.00
Impala horns	15.00
Waterbuck horns	17.00
(Others in proportion)	

Fullhead Rugs:
African cheetah	$105.00
African leopard	105.00
African lion, male	$120.00–150.00

Making Novelties Using Tanned Skins Belonging to Customer:

Zebra
Albums, for 8 x 10 photos, single	$ 35.00
Cigarette boxes to hold 2 to 3 packs	15.00
Wastebaskets	$ 55.00– 75.00
Hassocks	45.00– 75.00
Screens	200.00–350.00
Rugs, no feet	65.00– 85.00

Miscellaneous
Elephant tusks, bronze base and board for handing or standing	per tusk	$ 55.00
Elephant-foot metal-lined wastebasket or stool		55.00
Rhino-foot ashtray		20.00
Buffalo-foot ashtray		15.00
Elephant-foot ashtrays or trays		22.50
Elephant-ear map		150.00

P. ZIMMERMAN, SCULPTOR-TAXIDERMIST
PRICE LIST

Animal Species	Head & shoulder mount, any position	Dressing bodyskin aver. size
	Shs.	Shs.
Bongo	750/	190/
Buffalo (large mount)	975/	—
Buffalo (small mount)	900/	—
Bushbuck	395/	45/
Cob	420/	60/
Dik-dik	175/	7/
Duiker	175/	28/
Eland bull	975/	300/
Eland cow	850/	250/
Gerenuk	395/	40/
Grant's gazelle	395/	45/
Greater kudu	925/	175/
Hartebeest hunters	475/	80/
Hartebeest hacksons	495/	95/
Hartebeest Lichtenstein	475/	85/
Hyrax	—	3/50
Impala	395/	45/
Klipspringer	175/	25/
Kongoni	475/	85/
Lechwe (Mrs. Grey)	495/	55/
Lesser kudu	475/	45/
Oribi	175/	30/
Oryx	525/	95/
Puku	395/	45/
Reedbuck	395/	45/
Roan antelope	800/	125/
Sable antelope	875/	125/
Sing-sing (waterbuck)	600/	125/
Sitatunga	395/	45/
Steinbuck	175/	25/
Suni	120/	7/

P. ZIMMERMAN, SCULPTOR-TAXIDERMIST
PRICE LIST (*cont.*)

Animal Species	Head & shoulder mount, any position	Dressing bodyskin aver. size
	Shs.	Shs.
Thompson's gazelle	325/	30/
Tiang	500/	95/
Topi	475/	85/
Wart hog	525/	—
Waterbuck	525/	90/
Wildebeest	525/	125/
Zebra—common	750/	190/
Zebra—Grévy's	800/	200/
Rhino	1,350/	—
Aariwolf	250/	125/
Baboon	425/	275/
Badger	195/	125/
Hyena	425/	350/
Cheetah	450/	350/
Jackal	195/	125/
Leopard	45/	350/
Lion	875/	750/
Lioness	795/	600/
Otter	195/	125/
Serval cat	210/	100/
Wild dog	395/	265/

Antelope, Zebra, Rhino and Elephant Feet:

Buffalo, eland or zebra feet mounted as lampstand, table cigarette lighter, bookends (fitted on wood) or candlesticks, etc., according to design—

from Shs. 125/— upward

Rhino foot mounted:

as a cigarette box	Shs. 145/
as a cigar box	120/
as an ashtray holder	95/
as a doorstop	110/

Elephant foot mounted as stool, table or cocktail case, according to design—   from Shs. 295/   upward.
Elephant sole, mounted as a cocktail tray—

from Shs. 250/   upward.

Note: The shilling is equivalent to 14 cents.
20 shillings = 1 pound ($2.80).

CHAPTER XII

A PHOTOGRAPHIC SAFARI

Some people claim photographing animals can be every bit as exciting as bagging them. Of course, I am partial to hunting with rifle rather than a camera, although I have thoroughly enjoyed capturing on film the color and beauty of Africa's wild game.

In recent years, the photographic safari has gained in popularity. The outstanding advantage is cost. The photographic safari's crew numbers less men. There are not the costs of licenses, firearms and ammunition, trophies, and so on. You bring your film trophies home—and in the case of enlargements or the projection of slides, they adorn your walls. Your "trophy" room is truly magnificent, thanks to modern photographic techniques and equipment.

British East Africa has a right to be proud of her national parks and game preserves. Here, thousands upon thousands of game animals and birds roam at will, secure in their knowledge they are no longer in danger from the African tribesman (except poachers), the European settler, and the safari enthusiast.

Tanganyika used to have one of Africa's best-known havens for wild game, the Serengeti National Park, but the area was turned back to local African tribes, much to the consternation of game conservation enthusiasts. The park's most famous feature was the impressive Ngorongora Crater, where thousands of animals sought refuge each year. Visitors could either stay at the park's lodge at the lip of the crater, or they could venture down to the encircled valley and camp, provided a safari firm organized the trip. In Tanganyika today, the camera fan can still photograph all sorts of wild life, although he has not the advantage of heavy concentrations offered by Kenya's parks and reserves.

Uganda's two great national parks, Queen Elizabeth and Murchinson Falls, feature comfortable lodges, river cruises and all-day photographic safaris. Approximately one thousand elephants are in each park and many thousands of Cape buffaloes. Rhinos are not numerous, perhaps a fortunate thing for the park's visitors. They, more than any animal, cause the "tense moments." You will see prides of lions and an occasional leopard. The parks are abundant in the better-known species of antelope, gazelle, monkeys, birds, etc. Murchinson Falls Park has the ugly African crocodile and many hippos to photograph. One particularly interesting note about Uganda's national parks: the visitor can get out of a vehicle to photograph an animal, something unheard of in Kenya. Frankly, I tend to favor Kenya's strict safety rule on this subject.

Kenya has the greatest variety of national parks and game preserves in Africa. The National Park of Nairobi is the smallest of all faunal parks, slightly over forty square miles. The park is only five miles out of Nairobi and attracts over 100,000 visitors a year. The Tsavo National Park is the largest national park in the world and is over 8,000 square miles in area. Visitors stay at the park's three hospitable lodges. One unusual park feature is Mzima Springs. Visitors may photograph hippos and crocodiles through a glass-sided tank, some twenty feet long and six feet wide, actually immersed in the springs. The Amboseli National Reserve is 1,300 miles in area and is situated north of snow-capped Kilimanjaro, the highest mountain in Africa. The park is well known for its rhino and elephant population. There are many lion prides and the bird life is most colorful. Marsabit National Reserve is known for its variety of scenery and animals, the Kaisut Desert, the high volcanic plateau of Marsabit Mountain, numerous crater lakes and mountain ranges. Here you will see the gerenuk antelope and Grévy's zebra, found in no other area in Africa.

Animals in all the national parks and game reserves are rapidly accustoming themselves to their visitors and show little fear and less curiosity as man shoots wild game with his camera.

Kenya's park authorities have two principal rules. The visitor may not leave his car, and firearms are not allowed in these game conservation areas. The parks close at sundown, so check your petrol and the mechanical condition of your vehicle. I wouldn't relish the thought of a lion charge while changing a flat tire. If you do get stuck, for some reason, and the park's *askari* patrol has not detected your plight, spend the night in the car. Don't try pushing the car to a park exit. A rhino might elect to give you and car unsolicited aid.

So whenever you travel in Africa, and for whatever purpose, bring along that camera. Memories fade—negatives won't.

CHAPTER XIII

AROUND THE CAMPFIRE

There is a touch of magic about a safari campfire. A campfire relaxes a man's mind and warms his body. Clients and their professional hunters find it a center for pleasant conversation. And many times the crackling flames discourage conversation, permitting a man the chance to become absorbed in his own thoughts.

The campfire is the natural place to relate current and past hunting experiences. And questions are asked around a campfire—many questions.

I thought the final chapter should be devoted to some of these questions and I will try the best I can to answer them. The answers are necessarily opinionated and yet I hope objective enough to give you a picture of safari life in Africa.

How Does a Man Become a Professional Hunter?

Practically all professional hunters are men who have spent the better part of their lives in Africa. The exception is notable, as is true in anything. A few "pros" had gone on safari as clients only to return to enter the profession. However, the great majority of hunters are men whose fathers were either professional hunters or who were raised on farms and plantations in Africa and chose hunting as their livelihood.

All professional hunters must work hard to become members of the East African Professional Hunters Association. They are first assigned as camp assistants. In this capacity, they are given more and more additional responsibilities, but always supervised by an association member. Competent outfitting firms must be assured that their hunters understand people as well as animals. Once a firm feels their apprentice hunter is suited to take out clients, he is graduated to the position of junior hunter. Men with more experience, referred to as senior hunters, take the junior hunters in tow and continue their training. I might add, you're as safe with a junior hunter in the East African Professional Hunters Association as you are with "senior" hunters throughout the rest of the world.

The life of a professional hunter is not an easy one. Besides being a host, confidant and protector, he is an accomplished organizer. Consider for yourself what his average working day is like. He's the first one up in the morning, raising hell with the safari crew because fresh campfires have not been built. He visits the mess tent and sees to it the cooks are preparing a first-rate breakfast. He checks the entire crew to make sure no one has wandered off in the middle of the night in search of "African brew" or a young damsel. (This does happen occasionally.) During the hunter's early morning camp staff meeting, the safari boys are given their individual work instructions for the day. There's a firewood detail, water detail, cleanup detail, and so forth. There may have been a client's complaint about the daily laundry or a tent boy forgot to fill a kerosene lamp. Perhaps the portable shower isn't working properly. The cook says he is low on starches. A driver needs a new spring for the truck. The head boy can't fix the water filter. The skinners need more salt to cure the hides. A client's rifle stock has a split in it. These, and many more daily problems, must be solved promptly and efficiently by the professional hunter before the client has his morning fruit juice.

Then the hunter spends the entire day with his client in search of game. At the end of the hunting day, they return to camp where the exhausted safari sportsman soaks away his aches in a canvas tub of hot water. Meanwhile the exhausted hunter checks to see that the camp is in order. Rifles cleaned by the gunbearers are personally inspected by the hunter. Local trackers are paid their day's wages. Then the hunter visits the mess tent to organize the dinner. Next comes the "complaint session." Africans have personality clashes like anyone else. The safari boys air their differences before the hunter. The hunter raises a little hell with them and all is serene for a few days.

Now he must bathe (if there's time before dinner). Right about now, the client wants to know the whereabouts of his hunting companion. The hunter's presence is requested because a drink isn't the same without him. After dinner, there is the campfire session where the hunter is expected to relate tales about Africa and hunting experiences. Soon the client's eyes begin to droop. He excuses himself and retires for the night.

The hunter's day is not over with yet. There are trophies to be tagged, and the skinners' work to be inspected. The drivers and their vehicles are next on the list. How's the petrol supply holding out, and what about the condition of the tires? Local trackers are waiting patiently around the campfire to be questioned about new game movement. Their answers may decide a change of plans for the following day's hunt.

Then, the professional hunter sits down with his "homework," a series of game department forms to be filled out, recording what animals have been shot that particular day. Petty cash is counted and its usage is recorded for the safari firm. One more tour around camp to see that everything is in proper order, and the hunter can finally lie down on his cot for a few hours' rest.

Now I have a question: How many of you want to lead the "romantic" life of a professional hunter?

How Long Does the Average Safari Last?

The average African safari takes thirty days' time. Before World War II, safaris were mostly limited to wealthy international sportsmen. Their safaris lasted several months at least, because time and expense were of little consequence to the select few. Presidents of business firms, members of the international society set, and royalty mostly enjoyed the pleasures of safari life.

Since the war, standards of living have risen considerably. More people can afford to go on safari. Also, safaris aren't as expensive as they used to be. Safari outfitting has become big business, and prices are competitive. Other conditions have aided in the increased popularity of safaris. Modern air travel has solved the time problem. Also the "fly now, pay later" airlines' credit program has enticed many people to Africa.

Many people can afford safari but cannot afford a long leave of absence from their business, a principal reason the average safari takes only thirty days. Besides, should the sportsmen bring along the family, their wives, mothers, mothers-in-law, sisters and daughters are generally not too enthusiastic over stomping through the bush for more than a month, particularly if it is going to take away from time allocated for stopover visits in Rome, Paris, London, Copenhagen, etc.

Actually, it is surprising to see how many women do go on safaris today. There have been many theories suggested, but the few that make sense to me are: (1) The old lady wants to have hubby see Paris through her eyes and no one else's. (2) A compromise on that European trip. She and daughter will tag along in the bush, if he'll tag along with them down Europe's fashionable shopping promenades. (3) There are those women who are genuinely interested in whatever their husbands do, and want to share his pleasures.

How Long Should a Safari Last?

The ideal hunting safari should take a minimum of forty-five days, and nearer sixty days of actual hunting for sportsmen who wish first-class trophies. Thirty days is a minimum required time to bag a fair selection of game, but don't expect any world records. Thirty days is more than ample time to "slaughter" the majority of animals permitted on a general license.

If this sounds unappetizing to you, consider how revolting it is to professional hunters, game wardens, and park rangers. It is true that entirely too many people come to hunt Africa in order to show their friends back home that they have accomplished a daring, dangerous feat and henceforth should be referred to as the great white hunter in their social and business circles. They are completely unaware of the meaning of sportsmanship and challenge. Their paramount thought is "How many heads can I put up in the trophy room?"

In thirty days' time, they can shoot a lot of animals and,

unfortunately, there are no hunting laws in existence today that can suppress this type of client. Yes, we do have hunting laws that prohibit the shooting of certain female species, and there are laws which state that only "mature" males can be killed. Yet the term "mature" is not specific enough to prevent unreasonable shooting.

For instance, in some cases it is illegal to shoot an elephant whose ivory is less than twenty pounds per tusk. The type of client I refer to as a butcher rather than a sportsman will shoot the first elephant he sees whose tusks are in the twenty-to-thirty-pound category. He figures that he only has a certain time in Africa and he must have that picture of himself sitting on top of an elephant. After all, what do the people back home know about twenty-pound tusks or eighty-pound tusks? An elephant is an elephant, isn't it? Or so his too-eager mind reasons.

Now take the sportsman. He knows that it might take him thirty days to forty-five days before he will see a trophy elephant. By that, I mean a mature bull whose tusks are seventy pounds upwards. It is the dream of every sportsman who has hunted elephant in Africa to bag a hundred-pounder. There are not that many elephants left in Africa which have this heavy ivory, and only a few hundred-pounders are taken each year.

One thing is for certain: Short of a miracle, trophies of this caliber are taken only by the sportsman. Why? Simply because he has taken the time to hunt down that one particular trophy. He has exposed himself to all the unpleasant elements which generally accompany hard hunting. He is actively pursuing his challenge from sunup to sundown, and oftentimes camps along the trial so that he may pursue his quarry at sunup the following day. He'll see hundreds of elephants

and all of them quite adequate, but he knows, as all sportsmen know, that the satisfaction of hunting something less
than a trophy is merely a compromise with his own set of
ideals. Fortunately, sportsmen do not compromise.

Whether it is hunting elephant or any other animal, the
same principles are involved. One can't count on thirty days to
hunt the elusive bongo, the rare sable antelope or the much-
sought-after lesser and greater kudu. These animals are considered trophies because they must be hunted on their own
terms. The rough terrain, the heat, the stinging tsetse fly, and
the scarcity of the animal cause the sportsman many sleepless
nights. Yet all these things are well worth the one moment
when a trophy is bagged in a sportsmanlike manner.

It is a great deal easier to shoot than not to shoot. A man
knows he is a sportsman when he can enjoy seeing animal life
pass before him (none of trophy caliber) and not have the
slightest reluctance to return to camp without firing a shot.
This is why I claim one must be on safari for at least forty-five
to sixty days in order to offset Lady Luck's fickleness and the
law of averages.

Perhaps this is one reason that Africa calls sportsmen back
to hunt again and again. The more one sees of this gigantic
continent, the more one realizes how much he has missed
before. And sportsmen are truly the only ones who return to
Africa. Those individuals who belong to "Killers Incorpo-
rated" have accomplished their purpose in thirty days of indiscriminate shooting.

The man who cannot afford more than thirty days of safari
life at one given time should really plan Africa in two trips if
finances permit. Then he is not fighting a time element, and
is bound to end up with a formidable list of trophies.

People Returning from Safari Claim They Were Jinxed by a Certain Animal. What About This Jinx Idea?

Generally speaking, each hunter has his own special "jinx." I go one better than that. I have already talked about my greater kudu jinx in a previous chapter. But I did not mention my zebra jinx. To me, a zebra is like a horse with painted stripes; actually not so very far from the truth. I expect my extreme affection for horses makes me a bit squeamish when I take aim at a zebra.

Some men say they are jinxed by one or several of the Big Five—lion, leopard, rhino, Cape buffalo, and elephant. They claim something always seems to "spoil their kill" at the last moment. More than likely, their anxiety to conquer their subconscious or conscious fear of these dangerous opponents suggests careless hunting habits. They may make too fast an approach and spook the animal. Extreme nervousness causes unnecessary hand movements and the clearing of a throat or a cough. Often they attempt a desperation shot, rather than wait for a sure kill because "they want to get the whole thing over with." Some men tremble slightly when they are about to shoot a member of the Big Five. I might add, this is nothing to be ashamed of. It takes experience and a disciplined mind to remain completely calm during a charge from one of these "roughnecks."

Then there are people who list the rarer-type animals as their jinx. They do not take into consideration the general scarcity of the animals as well as their extreme alertness, excellent vision and hearing, and natural camouflage adaptability. I refer to the greater and lesser kudus, sable antelope, bongo, oryx, and sitatunga.

One day a chap from Mexico City cornered me in the New

Stanley Hotel bar and complained bitterly, over gin and tonics, that the sable antelope was his jinx. I listened patiently and silently for an hour. Finally I asked him how many sable antelope he had ever seen. His reply was, "One for sure, and I thought I saw half another one." Well, now, I cannot honestly agree that the sable antelope can be called this man's jinx. I'll go along with the fact that the gentleman from Mexico had experienced bad luck in not being able to see more sable antelope. Yet I wonder whose fault this was. Remember the old saying: "Seek and ye shall find."

Is There Any Restriction About Where We Can Hunt?

Most safari organizations book hunting areas in advance for their clients. This is done in the interests of game conservation as well as the client's safety.

There must be control of hunters if there is to be control of game. If such were not the case, thirty safaris could arrive at the same time in one hunting area unbeknownst to all concerned. The results would be much the same as the Allied landing on Anzio beachhead. Entire pockets of game would be literally wiped out, not to mention the number of hunters who would be playing harps instead of cards. Therefore, only one safari at a time is allowed to be in any one given specific hunting area.

These areas are plotted out on the Game Department's master map. Professional hunters try to present their safari plans well in advance to the Game Department. They reserve a game area best suited to the client's trophy needs.

Quite often the hunter will request an area and find that it has already been booked by another hunter. He must then pick another available game area. It would be well for the potential safari client to keep this fact in mind. The client should co-operate with his safari outfitter fully and let the organization know at the earliest possible moment when he wishes to go on safari (exact dates), and the type of game he wishes to hunt. There is no better insurance for a successful safari.

Different species of wild game are indigenous to certain terrain and climate. That is why one hears the terms "rhino country," "elephant country," "lion country," and so forth.

Plains-game animals do not present too big a hunting problem because of their abundancy throughout Kenya and Tanganyika. However, such is not the case when one wishes to go after less attainable game, such as sable, kudu, sitatunga, bongo, rhino, lion, leopard, elephant, and so forth. The above-mentioned animals do not roam at random throughout Africa. These worthy trophies are diminishing at an alarming rate and would face extinction without the continued conscientious hard work of British East Africa's Game Departments and Departments of National Parks.

There are game rangers assigned to specific hunting areas and each game ranger has native *asakaris* under his command to help carry out the best interests of game control. These men keep a careful vigilance over the movement of animals inhabiting their specific area.

At one time, nature maintained the ideal balance control but in recent years the laws of nature have become unbalanced. African tribal communities are expanding into areas heretofore uninhabited. Native poachers have formed organized smuggling rings. White settlers have farmed new land tracts. Therefore, Africa's wild game is being disturbed by Caucasian and African alike. The Game Department officials wisely exercise their authority when they see the normal propagation of herds is diminishing because of these disturbances.

Presently, there are areas in Africa that are closed for three to five years, in order to give game animals a chance to "settle down" and resume peaceful living habits.

After an area has been closed for the predetermined length of time, Game Department officials usually reopen it, providing there is once again an abundance of animal life.

Which Animals Face Extinction?

In my estimation, the two most sought-after animals facing possible extinction are the lion and the rhino. Other game species' numbers have seriously dwindled as well. I shall list these animals and birds, partially protected by game laws, so that the reader may better sense the alarm felt by British East Africa's game conservationists. They are as follows: the leopard, elephant, colobus monkey, blue monkey, ostrich, Grévy's zebra, giant forest hog, klipspringer antelope, oryx antelope, mountain reedbuck, sitatunga antelope, gerenuk gazelle, greater and lesser kudu, tree hyrax, Abbot's duiker antelope, caracal, serval cat, sable antelope, Sharp's grysbok gazelle, and the rock rabbit.

As this book is being written, the East African Game Department, the Department of National Parks, and the East African Professional Hunters Association are championing game conservation. The gorilla (Belgian Congo), cheetah, giraffe, and the greater bustard bird—alarmingly scarce—are completely protected.

All animals in numerical minority cost more money to hunt. In past years, the prices of special game licenses have increased considerably. The reader should be aware that this increase is in the best interests of animal conservation and is not part of an inflationary movement, as has been suggested by some people totally ignorant of the facts. While these extra tariffs may not seem fair to the prospective safari client, he must realize that Game Department decisions are not made by impulse, rather from carefully studied facts on animal population.

The problem of game conservation has become so serious in recent years that even Africa's most common game is protected. Game licenses specifically state the type and number of animal species that each license holder is allowed to shoot.

There is one important point to bring out when discussing game conservation. The person responsible for Africa's diminishing wild game is the African himself.

The most serious problem Game Department authorities face each day is the African poacher. I am not introducing this subject to create a political furor, yet I feel it is only justice to the East African Professional Hunters Association to state the facts. Safari outfitting firms have been blamed heedlessly for the disappearance of African game. There are thousands of Africans who conscientiously work with Game Department officials. They have shown intelligence and understanding of the problem, but unfortunately their numbers are equaled by those Africans who have not.

"Poacher" is a word used to refer to a person who unlawfully takes the life of game. Africans disobey Game Department rules for several reasons. There are those natives who kill wantonly because of the monetary gains they can derive from rhino horns, elephant ivory, and the better-quality antelope and gazelle skins.

Then there are those Africans who resent any type of rules or regulations the Game Department sets forth. They feel no government administration has the right to change the living habits enjoyed by them and their forefathers. While at first glance their viewpoint may have an element of moral justification, one must realize that there would be no need of any game restrictions if conditions were the same now as they were in past generations. Therefore, we must consider this type of African as a menace to wild life conservation. Too often their senseless killing of game is their method of defiance to administration.

There is the group of Africans who kill game wantonly and camouflage these acts under the pretense of fear. Let us say an African community moves from one area to another, a frequent occurrence. Naturally these Africans build new dwellings and farm new land. In order to feel secure in their new home, the young warriors search the area for possible dangers. If this area has not been inhabited recently by other African tribes, the newly established African community is reasonably sure to find heavy concentrations of game. The Africans reason that they would be safer if all game were cleared from the area, and so begins their illegal hunting.

I can understand why natives would be disturbed if such an area were filled with rhino, lion, leopard, elephant, and Cape buffalo. After all, no farmer appreciates his crops' being destroyed by rampaging elephants. I can further see why Africans would be reluctant to live in an area where hungry lions could attack them once they strayed from their village enclosure. Nor would anyone filling a water bag by the river appreciate a sudden introduction to a rhino horn.

So what can be done under circumstances such as these? All the African community has to do is to send word to the game ranger in his area. The ranger and *askari* will promptly solve their problems. These rangers, with years of experience, know how to move the dangerous animals out of an area without unnecessary slaughter.

Do the Africans contact the proper officials? No. They take matters into their own hands and start a campaign of eliminating wild game. Natives and animals alike are killed and very little else is accomplished, except the breaking of sound game laws.

However, the underlying fact is that Africans don't regulate their slaughter to the potentially dangerous species of animals. They'll kill anything that moves, whether they use bow and arrow, spear, traps, snares and, wherever allowed, antiquated firearms.

On different occasions, I have seen villagers try to convince game authorities that they killed antelope and gazelle to protect the community. The villagers' story had one point in common; they didn't believe their alibi, the Game Department didn't believe it, and heaven knows the slaughtered animals knew better. In fact, most Africans (other than poachers) kill game indiscriminately because of their love of meat.

Game Department authorities are not so naïve as to think they can prevent Africans from killing animals for food, but they know that they must also enforce laws to control this native pursuit of game. Discriminate killing is one thing, and indiscriminate slaughter is quite another.

Wild game does have a chance to survive in Africa, provided sportsmen and Africans give the Game Department their much-needed respect and co-operation.

Here's a question often asked by the fairer sex:

*What About Bugs, and Is There Any Guaranteed Repellent
Available on the Market?*

The man will make a fortune who invents a bug repellent
that works on all of Africa's flying insects. There are many
product claims; but to the best of my knowledge, there is no
repellent that has proven satisfactory in combating the vicious
bite of the tsetse fly. I realize that I have mentioned the
tsetse in a previous chapter, but this "beast" rates a few additional words.

I can think of no other winged creature which has created
more discomfort in Africa than this little monster. The tsetse
fly lives off blood and he's not particular whether he dines on
animals or human beings. In fact, I have always been suspicious of tsetse flies. They seem to know when I am hunting
in their area. At least the animals get a break when the tsetses
decide on me as their main course.

The tsetse's sting is not annoying, it's downright painful.
When they attack in groups, a man is driven beyond the limits of his patience. I have seen hunters, myself included, voice
more disreputable words at the tsetse fly than at a charging
rhino.

The heaviest concentration of wild game is in tsetse-fly
areas. The hunter must make one all-important decision. Can
he stand the aggravation? This may seem strange, but I have
seen people driven out of good hunting grounds because of
this "beast," no larger than your thumbnail.

Africa's animals would gladly sign a petition to get rid of
the tsetse fly because they suffer as much as people. However,
it is interesting to note that inadvertently the tsetse fly is
African wild game's best friend. As long as there are heavy
concentrations of tsetse flies, there will be heavy concentra-

tions of game, because natives refuse to live in tsetse-fly areas.

As for other insects and bugs of Africa, you hardly notice them, once you and Mr. Tsetse Fly have had your first encounter.

Mosquitoes, moths, gnats, etc., can all be dealt with by repellents. But the person on safari will come to a very astute realization after being in the bush twenty-four hours. There are more bugs in Africa than repellent in camp and no repellent has a utopian permanency.

In the final analysis, your best weapon will be your mosquito netting and an infinite amount of patience.

How Expert a Shot Do You Have to Be?

I would advise anybody contemplating a safari to become acquainted with as many calibers of rifles as is practicably possible. Time and again, safaris have ended up as failures because the client had not deemed it important to become better acquainted with firearms, particularly those of a heavier caliber.

Many valuable hunting hours and even days are lost on safari because of the indoctrination period essential for any client before he tackles big game. Naturally, a professional hunter will not permit his client to expose himself to any unnecessary and unforeseen dangers. Putting any weapon in the hands of a complete novice is a danger in itself. That is why professional hunters are insistent that a respectful friendship exist between rifle and client before they permit the client to face deadly game.

Potential safari clients do not have to waste so much valuable time if they acquaint themselves with rifle calibers up to and including the .375 Magnum, before they leave for Africa.

Once a person becomes confident in weapons of all calibers,

up to and including the .375, he should have little or no trouble in adjusting to the heavier-caliber rifles such as the .416 Rigby, the .458 Winchester, the .475 Holland & Holland, and in some cases the .500. However, it is not likely that anyone hunting in Africa will have to use a heavier caliber than the .470.

There is one rule to remember while hunting. The only shot that counts is your first one. The novice will quite naturally become excited when facing Africa's spectacle of game for the first time. Unfortunately, this excitement can sometimes dim a person's judgment and common sense.

The one thing a professional hunter hates to see is a wounded animal, and it happens every time when someone does not take his time and make absolutely sure that he is taking every advantage before shooting.

Only experienced sportsmen will occasionally venture a snap shot, and that is because they have complete confidence in their marksmanship. Most often they wait because they have seen wounded animals before, crashing blindly through thick brush. The animal's cries and the visual signs of his suffering is an experience that must etch itself permanently into a man's mind and conscience.

Naturally, there is the element of human error. Anyone can miss his intended target and wound an animal, but this happens rarely if the safari client does not allow greed, impatience, and lack of judgment to get the better of him.

There is an expression in Swahili, *poli poli*, meaning "slowly, slowly." Oftentimes, professional hunters and native gunbearers will repeat this quietly to the person who is stalking animals for the first time. There is a selfish motive behind these words of caution as far as the hunter and gunbearer are concerned; for, as you know, they are the ones who must risk their lives going after the animal *you* have wounded. It would be well for anyone hunting in Africa to remember this before squeezing the trigger.

How Will I Know Which Animal to Shoot?

Let me answer this question in a roundabout way. A vital factor to the successful continuance of East African game species is the assurance that game bloodlines do not stagnate. New blood is needed, so that inbreeding will not weaken or destroy a herd.

Nature has allowed a constant challenge between male animals. Only the strongest males dominate the herd. The reward for male supremacy is breeding choice of the female. The younger males have time on their side and they wait their chance knowingly. Time gives them stronger bodies, larger tusks and horns. When they feel time has rewarded them with a strength comparable to the herd leader, then the herd leader is challenged for his place of honor. Combat either gives this vied-for place of leadership to the younger male or the younger male leaves the battle nursing his wounds. In the latter case, impatience overshadowed discretion and the original herd leader continues to reign supreme.

Now what has all of this to do with hunting? A wise sportsman will stalk a herd diligently, review all the animals in the group before choosing his shot. His choice invariably will be an animal worthy of trophy classification—usually the herd leader, referred to above. The sportsman knows that once the herd bull has been killed, other males are eagerly waiting to take his place. And thus, new blood is introduced to the herd.

Also when hunting, one should be on the lookout for the sick animal or the animal that has obviously outlived his usefulness. These animals have been expelled by the herd because of their age or they leave voluntarily because they know death is imminent. Most such animals make magnificent trophies.

In any case, do not shoot a female, and discipline yourself to pass up the young males who have yet to reach their prime of life. Admittedly, some of these males make presentable trophies. But there are others just as good—and much older.

Around the campfire, the questions and answers lead to anecdotes collected over years of hunting by the white hunter. I have brought together some of these wonderful stories for you in this book. But there's no time like the present to begin your own collection.

Exciting Africa, with its promise of good company and good hunting, awaits. There are no thrills like the thrill of the hunt. There are few pleasures like those of the company of friends around a campfire. There are few rewards like those of the exercise of skill.

Whether your "weapon" is camera or rifle, the challenge is there—and the prize. See you on safari?